IF YOU
BUILD IT
WILL THEY COME?

IF YOU BUILD IT WILL THEY COME?

Three Steps to Test and Validate
Any Market Opportunity

ROB ADAMS

WILEY

John Wiley & Sons, Inc.

CONTENTS

Chapter Seventeen

Chapter Eighteen

Chapter Nineteen

Chapter Twenty

Chapter Twenty-One

Chapter Twenty-Two

Market Validation

Why Ready, Aim, Fire *Beats* Ready, Fire, Fire, Fire, Aim

If you've picked up this book, you have a new product on your mind.

You're working with an established company and looking to launch a new offering; you're a new company trying to muscle its way into a market; or you're a savvy business person trying to figure out more about the markets around your existing products.

Regardless of the seat you're sitting in or the time frame you're looking at, you're searching for every advantage you can find. You want to blow the market away with your offering.

WHY YOU NEED TO READ THIS

If any of these descriptions fit you, let me tell you why you need this book. More than *65 percent* of new products fail. And that's just in established companies with other established products and deep resources. If we switch over to start-ups, the failure rate takes a huge leap to *90 percent*. The amazing part is that we're not looking at data related to recessions or other tough business circumstances. These numbers have been stubbornly constant for 30 years.

Here's the bottom line: These numbers are simply not acceptable by any measure, especially when you multiply the failure rates by the money invested in research and development every year all around the world. Do the math and you'll get and annualized investment in failed products of $260 billion in the United States alone. Expand this worldwide and new product failures add up to trillions of dollars; dollars right down the drain. What a phenomenal waste of time, effort, capital, and business resources.

This book addresses the issue head-on. It will show you how to cut *your* chance of failure. It's not a magic bullet—just a big step toward significantly improving the likelihood you'll succeed. Neither is it a theoretical method—but it is a pragmatic system I've used with great success.

The process is Market Validation. It's a series of common business practices assembled in a unique way that prove the validity of a market *before* you make the product investment.

The concept was introduced in my first book, *A Good Hard Kick in the Ass: Basic Training for Entrepreneurs* (New York: RandomHouse/Crown, 2002). In that book, I covered Market Validation basics in one chapter. The response to that treatment has been significant, with demand coming from around the world for speaking and consulting on the topic which has continued since that book was published. The continued interest and demand have led me to write a book exclusively dedicated to Market Validation.

As you will see, there is nothing esoteric or magical about the Market Validation process. Like everything in business, there are no easy answers; if there were, business would be easy, and all new products would flourish. Conceptually, Market Validation is easy to understand—but it takes discipline and effort to get it done.

It is most important to remember that regardless of whether you are designing, building, or selling products, whether you're in a large corporation or a tiny start-up, or whether your business is service or product based, Market Validation will significantly increase the likelihood your product will succeed in the market.

Before we delve into Market Validation and all it encompasses, let's take a brief look at a key question: Why do products fail?

They fail because they don't generate enough money, enough revenue—of course. But why don't products generate enough revenue?

Because they don't sell well enough. Customers aren't willing to pay for them. Customers feel they're not compelling enough or not worth the value, given the price. They can't generate enough revenue to cover their expenses. Not, as many urban legends suggest, because the parent company or outside investors won't fund them. As an experienced investor and former corporate executive, I can assure you that corporations and investors will back promising products and services that show market traction. But companies have to prove customers *want* the products for this to happen.

Clearly, if a company's first product fails, that's the end. If a new product fails in an established business, the company may or may not survive; it all depends on the strength of other revenue streams and on how many resources were burned on the failed product.

The theme here bears repeating: A company fails because it doesn't sell enough product or services. Outside investors or a parent company might cover shortfalls for a while, but ultimately, the offering must stand on its own. It must generate returns that justify the capital—and the risk—that went into creating, marketing, and selling it.

So, whether you're in a start-up or an established business, if you want your company to succeed, you need to consistently get your product or service offering right.

And if you want to know how to get your products and services right, follow the advice in this book. Use Market Validation to probe, test, and validate your market opportunity—*before* you invest all that money in product development. It is a systematic, proven approach. And it will make or break your business.

WHY MARKET VALIDATION MATTERS NOW, MORE THAN EVER

The majority of jobs in today's economy fill some role in the designing, building, or selling of products or services. The ubiquity of these three business functions to business careers is driven by the global economy and the dizzying array of products and services now available in our business and consumer lives. These choices are great news to us as consumers on the personal and business products fronts. On the flip side, as suppliers of these products or services, we are put constantly on point to understand the dynamics of the markets we serve.

In today's global economy, the rules have changed dramatically. During the twentieth century, manufacturing capabilities were frequently a company's source of competitive advantage. Market knowledge mattered, but the ability to effectively design and subsequently manufacture products was the key to serving markets, and these were relegated to larger organizations because of the large amount of capital required. Market knowledge was secondary and came with the territory of the vertical integration needed to service markets.

Twenty-first-century rules are considerably different. The global economy and the efficiency that it brings with it have made outsourcing an integral part of any effective company's strategy. If you've discovered a market need, you can outsource the design and manufacturing of the product or service to meet that market demand. No longer are design and manufacturing proprietary to large companies. If you can find strong market demand, your only real constraint is access to the capital that can buy the design and manufacturing services.

Clearly, this dramatically changes the rules of enterprise. Now, insight into a market is what matters. It is the new competitive advantage. Find me a market that is interesting, and I will find a way to build a product to serve that market.

How can you uncover market demand and use that knowledge to your advantage? That's exactly what this book is about. It provides a systematic framework that will help you develop an objective and realistic assessment of the market. In the end, the ultimate proof of your market is getting buyers to open their wallets and part with their money. Market Validation is a system that mimics that process without risking all the capital it takes to build the product.

THE IRIDIUM EXAMPLE

My favorite example of the need for Market Validation is best illustrated by Iridium, a satellite-based phone system from the 1990s. I've used this example on a regular basis for years, because I think it best illustrates the need for Market Validation. It also shows how big companies with strong industry backing and experienced investors can easily be led astray from understanding the fundamentals of their markets when faced with stimulating business and technical challenges.

Iridium was conceived in the late 1980s as a worldwide, voice-based phone system and an alternative to existing copper telephone line and cellular phone systems. The idea was to put in place a low-earth-orbit satellite system to deliver the same phone services that cell and copper line systems did.

These satellites were placed to blanket the earth for global coverage. Given that the satellites had to communicate both with each other and with ground stations and Iridium handsets on the ground, the system originally was thought to require 77 satellites—the same number of electrons as the Iridium atom, hence the name. Since radio waves can only travel in a straight line, the satellites had to be placed in orbit in such a way that one satellite could always see another to relay its phone call.

These technical challenges, along with many others, were clearly daunting. Not only was there the expense of building and putting into orbit all those satellites, but there was also the technical challenge of building the satellites to survive in the austere conditions of space, getting all the programming right, and enabling the satellites, ground stations, and headsets to talk to each other. The company also faced the innumerable legal and regulatory challenges of building out a system in the highly regulated telecommunications industry that cut across countries and continents in a way that had never been done before. In the end, all these significant technical, regulatory, and business challenges were overcome. The system went live in the early 1990s. There was just one problem—a big one: Nobody called.

The original design target for the system had been the international business traveler, who Iridium thought would pay a premium for a single phone number and single voice mailbox that worked anywhere in the world. Based on my experience working with companies developing products, I'm sure the company analyzed that market to size how big it was, then ran a number of models to forecast how much revenue could be generated. But I strongly suspect they stopped there, because there are more than a few shortcomings of the target market analysis that could have been easily overcome using fundamental Market Validation principles.

Before going into what Market Validation techniques could have been used here, let's look at some of the product characteristics of the Iridium phone system and contrast those with its target market.

First, as the system was being designed and built, from the late 1980s to early 1990s, cell phone usage in business was fairly ubiquitous. Even in the United States, with its older, analog-based system of the time, cell phone handsets were small and could fit in shirt pockets. Also at the time, a worldwide business traveler could get worldwide cell phone coverage using three different cell phones to get coverage on the three different cell phone infrastructures that existed at the time. It's doubtful that business users would need coverage in areas not covered by cell phone or copper lines, such as in the middle of the ocean or in remote wilderness areas. Given this, I would suggest that the Iridium system's competition within its stated target market was the usage and cost of three different cell phones the business traveler would need for worldwide coverage—if indeed their market hypothesis was correct to begin with.

The next step is to compare how the Iridium system stacked up with its competition (this again assumes the stated target market was accurate). This comparison, to put it bluntly, came out poorly. It's important to highlight that these shortcomings could have easily been known before the company spent the billions necessary to put the system in place.

The first big issue was the handsets. The initial versions were large and bulky and came with a briefcase full of attachments that had to be inserted into the headset, depending on where the phone was being used. It also had a 200-page operator manual and talked of the user's dexterity being important to using the system. Not a good way to compete with cell phones.

The second major issue involved all those satellites and the distance the phone calls had to travel to be relayed up from the ground, thrown across a bunch of satellites in space, and then returned to the ground. The sheer distance the signals had to travel meant there was a Houston-to-space-station propagation delay, making it impossible to have an interactive conversation. You had to pretty much say "over" when you were finished talking, wait for the person at the other end to hear what you said, then wait for them to respond and say "over" to indicate it was your turn to respond. Not a good way to compete with cell phones.

A third major issue was the fact that the phone could not be used indoors. Yes, that's right: In an age when cell phones had been around for quite a while, Iridium did not consider the fact that the satellite signals could not penetrate buildings. To work, the handset had to have a clear line of sight to the sky and the satellites in it. This also meant the phones could not work outdoors in urban areas where buildings blocked the sky.

The last point I want to emphasize is the system's cost and operating expense. Initially, you had to buy the handset for several thousand dollars, attend two days of training on how to use it (and remember all those different configurations it needed to be used in various places), and then pay for calls at anywhere from 5 to 10 times what a cell call would have cost.

There were other significant drawbacks to the system, but these are some of the major ones. I highlight them for the simple reason that Iridium could easily have understood these shortcomings before any development work was undertaken. The fact that the system wouldn't work indoors and would have a propagation delay could have been grasped in your average high school physics class; even at the speed of light, if the distance is far, you will have a delay, and radio waves from that far up in space don't have the energy to go through a building. The need for a complex handset configuration to communicate with the satellites and base stations could also have been understood, given the complexity of the electronics to make the system integrate.

I speculate that the bottom line on the Iridium experience was a tendency I see a lot of companies display. Give them a challenging technical or business problem, and they will rise to the occasion and overcome it. But ask them to define a target market, come up with a set of compelling features, and build a market-oriented solution, and many business people know they want it but aren't sure how to do it. This book is about doing all of this before you invest in an Iridium—only to have no one use the system.

Back to the Iridium story. How could Market Validation techniques have been used to uncover these issues before building the product? Motorola and some significant telecommunications-systems companies backed the original investment. Surely these people had the talent necessary to know if this would work.

This book will go through the entire process of Market Validation, which certainly should have been followed, given the $5 billion investment Iridium required. For now, let me highlight two methods that could have been used to validate this market before building the product.

The first would have been a survey pointed at the proposed target market of international business travelers: a simple survey—given in person, over the phone, or even electronically—pointed at 100 people in our target market of international business travelers. The purpose of this survey would not be to see if they wanted the Iridium system but to better understand their usage patterns and how they currently handled international phone calls for business.

A sampling of the questions would look like this:

How many days a year do you travel internationally?

When you travel internationally, how to you handle phone communications?

How much do you spend annually on international phone communications?

Would you find it valuable to have one phone number at which to be reached when travelling internationally?

Would you be willing to pay a premium for one international phone number?

If yes, how much would that premium be?

In my experience doing Market Validation work, this would give us a very strong early indicator of the pricing premium, if any, that international travelers would be willing to pay for this one-number, all-access service. This would not be a final indicator of price by any stretch but an early indicator of what kind of premium the user would be willing to pay versus his or her current system. In the line of questioning, we captured both how he or she handled international calling currently and how much it cost; we went on to ask how much of a premium he or she would be willing to pay. Simple but powerful stuff.

Armed with the data, we would have a baseline to compare what the target audience currently pays and what premium they would be willing to pay (both captured in the customer survey). This could be measured against the cost of the substitute system then in use including service with three different cell phone infrastructures. We then would have estimated the cost of our services based on the amount of money required to build the system.

Experience would suggest that in the surveys, respondents would come back willing to pay some premium for one-number international access, but it is doubtful it would have been more than the cost of coverage that was available as a substitute for the Iridium system at the time, which was three times the then current cost of cell phone coverage. Given that the implemented cost of Iridium was 5 to 10 times the cost of a cell phone call, the company clearly missed the mark here. Even if it wasn't sure what the final cost would have been early in the process, they could have easily known, based on substitutes, that to be competitive, they could not exceed the cost of the substitute or three times the cost of cell phone usage.

Following this user survey, I would have gone to a local lunch spot popular with business people, armed with a clipboard and pen, ready to make an offer. My offer would have been based on what we knew about the Iridium system before it was built and would go like this. First, I would screen to find people who were international business travelers. If they made that screen, I would offer to pay their cell phone bill for the next three months, regardless of how many calls they made. In exchange, I would ask them to tape a brick to their cell phone (to approximate the size of the original Iridium handset) and to only use their cell phone outside (to approximate the indoor limitations of a satellite system). Then, I would show them their cell phone bill to represent their bill marked up by 5 to 10 times. Based on experience, I seriously doubt I would have had any takers.

Is this an overly simplistic example? Yes. It glosses over many complexities and subtleties that will be covered in depth later in this book. At the same time, it drives home the power, and the necessity, of Market Validation.

Let me provide a short postmortem on the Iridium story, just to reinforce several points made here.

Given the capital requirements of $5 billion to build the system and the few users the system actually generated, the company went through a few product changes in an attempt to address some of the product shortcomings. In the vernacular of Market Validation, I like to use the metaphor of *"Ready, Aim, Fire"* as the correct process as opposed to the typical *"Ready, Fire, Fire, Fire, Aim"* process most companies actually do. While Iridium tried valiantly to address these shortcomings while they were in the *Fire, Fire, Fire* step, ultimately the company was forced into bankruptcy by its creditors.

The company was purchased out of bankruptcy for half a cent on the dollar of the original investment. The new company was able to analyze the market and realized that the real market demand was around a submarket of the original target market. Real demand existed in remote areas without any phone communications, in disaster and war zones where the existing phone infrastructure was not functioning, and at sea as emergency communications backup for ships and ocean-based oil rigs. This new target market was willing to pay the premium for the system over the cost of cell phones, because they had no other option. So, in the end, the company had demand, just not at the level the original investment demanded in order to make a profit.

OTHER EXAMPLES OF THE NEED FOR MARKET VALIDATION

The need for Market Validation has shown itself in many ways across many industries. In many cases, companies pursued products or services based on accurate market research data. The problem was that they did not dig deeply enough into the details to understand the nuances of the market. Using a Market Validation framework, they performed the *Ready* phase but did not go on to push through the *Aim* and *Fire* steps.

The Ford Edsel is a famous example from the late 1950s. Ford was flush with cash from its successful Thunderbird offering and was feeling the pressure of multiple product families available from its competitors. It embarked on an aggressive market research campaign to develop a new division with flagship offerings that could satisfy a broad market segment. Extensive market research and focus groups were used, and the results drove the new car division's brands, features, and options.

The Edsel was developed in direct response to the market feedback it had so carefully collected. These features included many new and innovative offerings for the time. A new line of dealerships was developed to carry what would become the Edsel line from Ford. The company aggressively advertised the car and its innovative features before its availability. The car came out. And the car flopped.

The challenges? Like most products, many things were done well, and many things could have stood improvement. But ultimately, the market judges by voting with its money. The new features that were expressed in market research came out in a car that the consumer viewed as overpriced. The advertising that tempted consumers with a completely new offering came on a platform that looked like other Ford offerings and at a price point that was the same as other Ford offerings, confusing the target audience.

The Edsel conclusion, using a Market Validation prism? When offering consumers a new product, it's important not only to meet customers' product expectations but also to have significant differentiation or price performance to get consumers to switch over to a completely new offering. The Edsel offered neither and has gone down in the annals of business history as a buzzword for product failure.

New Coke provides another example of how analyzing broad market data can yield one set of conclusions that does not match what you can find when you go deep into understanding your market.

Coke was smarting from the Pepsi wars of the mid-1980s. In those, Pepsi would do blind taste tests of affirmed Coke drinkers to see if they could tell Coke from Pepsi. Pepsi would typically win these tests by a small margin. Coca-Cola had an understandably strong reaction to this campaign, feeling that they were losing share to a new generation of Cola drinkers based on Pepsi's sweeter taste, and their share numbers were starting to back up this view.

Coca-Cola's reaction was to reformulate its offering to a sweeter taste, what it saw as a key reason for its losing share to the younger Cola market that was actively forming its nascent brand preferences. The results were dismal.

The company suffered a significant negative reaction to the newly formulated taste in the market. Despite an expensive and well-crafted rollout campaign, market share plunged almost immediately. The company was in turmoil and under heavy pressure to react. It ultimately did, brought its original formula back, and eventually regained market share against Pepsi.

What happened here using a Market Validation prism? Yes, on the surface, the company would lose to Pepsi in a taste test—and the emphasis needs to be on taste test. If you dug beneath the taste test, you would find that sweeter cola drinks definitely have appeal in the first few sips; but most of the discrimination between a sweet Pepsi and a not-as-sweet Coke comes through over the course of consuming an entire glass of the drinks, not just on the first impression. So, Pepsi would win most taste tests, but Coke drinkers preferred that a beverage be less sweet over the course of an entire glass. Here again, it is always critical not to get stuck at the first level of data; you need to go deeper and understand the entire customer experience.

A similar experience on a less public scale occurred after the purchase of Tivoli Systems by IBM in the mid-1990s. Tivoli Systems was a scrappy start-up in the systems management space that built a strong user base and followed through its innovative framework. IBM purchased the company and for a while let it continue to operate on its own. Tivoli aggressively leveraged the IBM brand, experienced considerable growth in sales, and continued to release innovative products.

Over time, IBM began to assimilate more and more of the company in an attempt to mainstream the Tivoli culture and spark the larger company with the scrappy start-up's ethos. When left alone, Tivoli was great at leveraging IBM's resources; once the mainstreaming process began, Tivoli started losing some of its product innovation.

Talking to insiders, what you learn is that much of this had to do with the differences between how IBM and Tivoli conducted their market assessments and competitive intelligence in developing new products.

Within Tivoli, gathering market information and competitive intelligence was an integral part of the product team's life. They worked aggressively to assess the market and to understand, through direct interaction, customer issues and competitive products. This competitive analysis frequently involved sitting with customers who had competitors' products installed and understanding all the subtleties of how they used them and what they liked about them. In the eyes of the scrappy Tivoli start-up environment, there was no one else this critical function could be performed by.

Fast forward to postmerger, post-IBM-assimilation Tivoli. Analyzing markets, user requirements, and competitive offerings was now done by a centralized function that specialized in this service and that was outside of the group actually owning the product. The centralized group conducting this research was very capable and very dedicated. There were, however, two cultural attributes that could not be overcome with this type of structure.

The first attribute was the dagger-in-the-teeth, take-no-prisoners approach that permeated the Tivoli culture from its days as scrappy start-up. The product managers who analyzed potential new markets knew their livelihoods depended on getting their new products right, and they analyzed their markets with this same do-or-die intensity. They simply would not trust their livelihood to someone who was doing the analysis while never having to live by the conclusions.

The second attribute that did not transfer well was the competitive profiling. The IBM approach was to understand the features and functionality of a competitor and then strive to beat it by a reasonable margin of 20 to 30 percent more functionality. Really, this meant going head-to-head with an established player using 20 to 30 percent more horsepower. The Tivoli approach was significantly different. With a culture based on a scrappy start-up, they knew they would never have enough time or money to go head-to-head with anybody. So, they would beat competitors by going where the competitors weren't. They would stake out a new way of solving a systems management problem with a totally new approach and claim this as their territory. That way, they owned it and spent their limited resources educating the world on how much more efficient their approach was. This enabled a very effective way to claim leadership in a market with significantly less time and money than what a head-on approach required, It also made competitors position against Tivoli versus the other way around.

Again, using a Market Validation prism and diving below the obvious approach that all competitors can follow gives us a unique and proprietary view of the market, lets us set the ground rules, and tilts the playing field in our favor.

WHAT ARE THE BENEFITS OF MARKET VALIDATION?

The benefits of Market Validation are compelling, straightforward, and ultimately based on economics. Most companies follow a *Ready, Fire, Fire, Fire, Aim* approach to delivering their products or services. They develop the product they think the market wants and then ship it; it underperforms, so the company scrambles to fix it and then probably goes through the same build-ship, build-ship process multiple times until they run out of money or randomly hit a market need. Think of Yosemite Sam whipping out his gun and blasting away; eventually, he may hit the target, but it's only by accident. But in this case, each bullet represents a significant amount of money and opportunity spent on designing, building, and launching a product. The question is, can the company shoot enough bullets to eventually be right by random chance?

Market Validation provides a systematic way to evaluate the market opportunity before the investments are made in designing, building, and launching the product or service. Ultimately, you ship the right product the first time, deliberately, which increases the likelihood of revenue traction, which in turn generates the likelihood of a successful offering, which ultimately leads to a cash-generating business.

Another key benefit of Market Validation is that you are developing the right set of features for a targeted audience. Classic market research causes you to target a wide range of features for broad markets. Market Validation gets you to a *targeted* market faster, with a *narrower* feature set, to get a strong hold in a *portion* of the broader market. Your product is tightly targeted, you can enhance it quickly, and the targeted nature of your audience enables high-productivity sales and marketing efforts. From this base camp of success, you're in a position of strength to expand your markets.

Getting the product right and focusing on a tightly defined market also gets you closer to shipping on schedule. By focusing your feature set to a defined target market with Market Validation, you are able to address features needed by the majority of a clearly articulated market instead of trying to address a broadly defined market with lots of generic features that appeal to the average market but directly appeal to no specific market.

This defining of markets allows for a simplification of features and the objective prioritization of production schedules to reflect must-have features demanded by the market versus nice-to-have features that matter but are not critical to your target market's users.

Another attribute of a thorough Market Validation process is communicating what the market has said by documenting both the product and the delivery schedule. A frequent complaint between sales and marketing groups and the engineering teams that are designing and building the product is the lack of a defined and prioritized set of product features from marketing, coupled with the lack of a schedule from engineering.

With a full validation effort, a thorough product specification is developed based on an objective assessment of the market. From that product specification, a defined schedule with time and resource estimates can be developed. These items combined give management teams the ability to objectively make product decisions and enables them to objectively evaluate the options for the "Do you want it right, or do you want it Friday?" trade-offs that are made for any product as it comes to market.

A follow-through benefit of full product feature and delivery documentation is that customers can have a full understanding of the product. Even on paper, a full product specification is something your customer base can give you input on before the entire development investment is made. From these specifications, product mock-ups and prototypes can be developed and placed in the hands of your customer base for early feedback.

One of the most important benefits of a fully specified, fully costed, and customer-vetted product is that the sales and marketing team knows what it's getting and at what date it's getting it. The benefit of a known product with a known ship date is invaluable as the sales and marketing investment starts to be made. As we will see, a complete Market Validation effort includes budgeting and executing a full product launch, and this product specification and scheduling process is the first step in making that launch effort reliable and cost effective.

WHAT KIND OF COMPANY BENEFITS?

Because Market Validation techniques are focused outside of the producing company on the markets they intend to serve, companies of any size playing in any market can use them. In subsequent sections and chapters, I'll outline some of the minor differences in techniques across different industries and different-sized companies, but the key takeaway here is that the overall strategic approach is the same—and all companies benefit. There is no particular company demographic that is better suited than another, because the nature of the work is assessing the market opportunity. Assessing the market opportunity is a separate, externally focused effort that is indifferent to the company size or type that is doing the work.

LEVEL OF EFFORT—HOW LONG DOES IT TAKE, AND HOW MUCH DOES IT COST?

For any of you out there looking to start using Market Validation, the burning question right about now is, how much does it cost, and how long does it take? Here's the big picture.

You need to allocate 60 days of effort before you start building your product and 10 percent of your development budget to get the Market Validation work done. The logic behind these figures is simple. You are spending 10 percent of your product development budget up front to make sure the remaining 90 percent you spend is being spent right. If the product isn't going to work, you need to know with a 10 percent versus a 100 percent investment. Most companies choose the latter option. The 60 days is a small amount of time to invest to get things right; if you feel your market can't wait 60 days for you to start building your product right, I suggest you don't have a real opportunity to start with.

There are three parts to the process: *Ready, Aim,* and *Fire.* This book covers these three parts sequentially, with each part consisting of multiple chapters. Again, the front-end work for Market Validation takes 60 days to complete, and the investment equates to 10 percent of your product development budget. I will cover techniques in each of these sections that reduce the amount of money that needs to be spent if you are doing this as an adjunct project to your full-time job or are working inside a cash-constrained start-up.

Part 1 of Market Validation, *Ready,* is designed to be a quick assessment of the market fundamentals of the opportunity you're considering pursuing. It is really a triage to see if the market characteristics around size, growth rate, types of customer, industry life cycle, macrotrends, competitors, and other major characteristics match up with the expectations for your new offering's ambitions. The time commitment is two days of work and no significant hard dollar investment. The end result is enough data to make a decision around moving forward and investing more time and effort or dropping the idea and moving onto the next offering to test. This process is also an excellent framework for comparing multiple ideas to prioritize their market appeal.

Part 2, *Aim,* is an in-depth dive into specific market facts that build on the material from the *Ready* step. In *Aim,* we go much deeper into the market and analyze it using a systematic approach to gathering data in a way that lets us objectively measure and gauge the intimate details of the target market and the demand for the potential product or service offering. The goal is to find our own proprietary approach to addressing the market requirement. This cannot be done using outside data that everyone has access to, including our competitors, so we need to go deep with our own resources to access the true nature of the market pain we are addressing. At the finish of the *Aim* process, we have a detailed offering, we know the target audience, and we understand pricing and feature characteristics to take full advantage of the opportunity. This step is the most time- and resource-intensive part of the effort and represents the majority of the 60 days and 10 percent of the development budget cost allocation. If you're in a cash-constrained situation, I'll give you alternative ways of getting the work done that will require more of your time but a lower dollar investment.

Part 3, *Fire,* is taking all the information gathered in the *Ready* and *Aim* steps and making sure all the data and material work their way into the final product or service offering. *Fire* is not about a time or dollar commitment but represents a series of steps and management techniques that ensure all the investments made in the *Ready* and *Aim* steps make their way into the offering.

THE "OF COURSE I WOULD DO THAT" FACTOR

Right about now, I know where you're at—you've got a quizzical look on your face. Your reaction to what you've read so far is "of course I would do that" when building a new product. In many ways, you feel what you've read so far is a restatement of the obvious that any experienced business person would do when delivering a new product or service to the market.

The reality is quite different. Look no further than the product failure numbers we've reviewed. Why is this? There are myriad reasons behind it; let me outline what I feel are the more relevant explanations.

One of the more common excuses I come across when working with companies on this front is "we don't have time to do this." The company skips Market Validation in the interest of time, puts its foot on the product development gas, gets a product out the door, misses the market, scrambles, reloads its dwindled resources, ships another product, and on and on and on until the company runs out of money and resources. The reality is that you *do* have time to do it. If a market is so competitive that 60 days of thinking before you start executing is the only difference between success and failure, I promise that it's just not a lucrative market to begin with.

Another factor I explored in my first book is the difference between an "output" mentality and an "execution" mentality. Simply stated, output mentalities look at large volumes of things that can get done, particularly when launching a product. The sourcing of suppliers, negotiating of distribution deals, and constant measuring of efficiency and quality represent output mentalities. Everyone looks really busy, and they're working long hours on tasks that contribute little to market assessment and selling the new product.

Conversely, an execution mentality goes right to the core of the matter, which is this: What do I need to do to increase the value of my product in the market? Interviewing customers is not what most people get out of bed every morning dying to do, but in the end, it is the ultimate way to produce value in the market, and it is the sign of an execution mentality. So, get outside your comfort zone and figure out *now* if the product you're contemplating will get your customer base to open up their wallets and part with their money. Any competent business person realizes an investment of 10 percent of a product budget is a small price to ensure that the other 90 percent is going to a real market need.

I frequently refer to the "urban legends" of business. If you pick up stories in the media of successful new products, they read like preordained events that required nothing more than following a list of punch-list items and turning a crank, and voilà—a successful product offering. Much of this is promulgated by what I like to refer to as "business pornography" that's designed to make great product successes look like trivial pursuits when covered in the press. Unfortunately, the reality is quite different. Strong products take a phenomenal amount of hard work, perseverance, timing, and ultimately luck. Companies that do it well are like graceful Olympic athletes that faultlessly execute challenging athletic endeavors. The Olympians do so with such graceful simplicity as to make the feat look trivial. What you don't see is the four-plus years of practicing more than 40 hours a week that went into that single performance. Successful product offerings have to be thought of in the same way.

Another significant issue is the difference between theory and reality. In this book, I will always reinforce the way things are done with examples of how to do them. The theory of what is discussed here is very pragmatic and makes sense to anyone with business experience. But ultimately, this is a book, and you're probably reading it under fairly pleasant circumstances. When you return to your job on Monday morning after an enjoyable weekend and the real issues come up and you're putting out fires, all this material could be for naught if you don't go out and put it to work.

WHAT'S SO HARD?

So, why is all this work that seems so obviously necessary so hard to pull off?

We talked about one of the bigger issues—the difference between an output and an execution orientation. It's easy to look busy when building a new product, which is the output orientation. It's harder to create value, which is the execution orientation—but ultimately the one that pays off.

Market Validation requires you to step outside your comfort zone and talk to potential customers, suppliers, industry analysts, media people, and other resources in the ecosystem of the market you're about to enter. People with sales and marketing backgrounds are used to this, but those without the experience are not comfortable reaching out to target markets because of the high risk of rejection. In order to get this work done properly, you need to get comfortable reaching out to target audiences. Remember, rejection is a form of feedback, and if you're going to be rejected, you want to do it on 10 percent of your budget, not 100 percent.

One of the things that make the process hard is the nature of the sales- and marketing-oriented process of assessing the market versus the nature of developing products or services. Developing and delivering a product is a discrete set of steps with measurement points along the way that can be regularly evaluated. There is a starting point and the systematic addition of parts, materials, or services with regular points of evaluation that eventually result in a finished product or service. Market Validation is a process or framework giving you a structured approach to capturing the serendipitous requirements needed to produce a product that gets accepted by the market. The general management approach of carefully measuring large amounts of data does not directly translate here. The development process for any product or service is tangible and more measurable, in that it is easier to gauge a product's progress objectively through the designing and building phases than it is to measure the completeness of how well that design is responding to the market before it is actually shipped. So, comparing the nature of Market Validation and product development brings with it some latent differences.

Like I've said, Market Validation requires you to step outside your comfort zone. When getting a new product out the door, it's a lot easier to stay inside the factory and battle your way through the constant barrage of interesting challenges that come up during the development process. It's easy to feel like the valiant hero working diligently to further the product development process. Again, this is a false economy. The insider work needs to be done but creates less value than outsider work that further defines the market and identifies the features to meet it. A day in the factory slaying beasts feels more productive, but in reality, a day on the road meeting with potential customers will dramatically reduce the number of beasts that need to be slain—and will make it easier to objectively figure out how to slay them.

Many business people can have a condescending attitude toward the sales and marketing function. They view the function as either easy or a black art. Both cases are not true, and the reality is that sales and marketing, particularly in today's competitive world, is difficult to do well.

Let me describe a scenario that highlights this. It's one I've seen many, many times. A new product is under development. The company has probably relied on its instincts or its current customer base to design it (two things that should, as we'll learn later, be inputs to a multifaceted design effort but not the sole inputs). After multiple delays, the product is approaching its ship date, and the company gears up its sales and marketing efforts by staffing up those functions. So, we're about 30 days from shipping a product that was designed from a few sketchy data points, and the sales and marketing staff are just coming on board. Formula for disaster.

Here's what will happen. The product will launch, and because it's based on vague market definition and mercurial feature priorities, it will flop. The sales and marketing team, which had nothing to do with the design process, will be blamed and probably replaced. In will come a new team, and a new set of features with a new target audience will probably be developed, this time under extreme pressure to make this version work in the market—probably ending with the same outcome. The new sales and marketing team, again, usually has the failure laid at its feet. In reality, the product was doomed from the start based on the poorly defined market it was going after. If blame needs to be assigned, it probably lies at the feet of the team that developed the product in a vacuum. A bad product is a bad product, and no amount of sales and marketing talent or budget can fix it.

So, why does this scenario—the *Ready, Fire, Fire, Fire, Aim* scenario—constantly repeat itself? In addition to all the reasons previously cited, another is the lack of glamour around Market Validation; it requires a lot of work, as well as management discipline to stick with it and follow through, and it produces no instant answers. You will get the answers you need, and if you follow the process, they will represent what your market is after, but there is no magical book you can go to and look up the answers. You need to figure them out yourself, and the only way to do this is by investing time and effort.

SALES AND MARKETING AS A FACT OF LIFE IN TODAY'S WORLD

One of the more common attributes of companies large and small that I work with on Market Validation is the overwhelming tendency to see the new product development process as over once the product ships—kind of a throw-it-over-the-wall mentality: Research and development have done their part; now it's time for the sales and marketing team to do theirs.

As you've probably gathered at this point, this is not the reality of today's business environment. No product, no matter how useful, interesting, and compelling, can thrive in the market without a real sales and marketing effort both to launch it and to keep it in the forefront of its target audience for as long as it's available. That sales and marketing process needs to be developed in parallel with the Market Validation process and in fact is a natural outcome of it.

The rule of thumb I like to use in estimating budgets for launch and sales and marketing efforts is to allocate as much for the product's sales and marketing effort in the first year as you did for building it. This emphasizes the importance of not just building the product but of effectively getting it into the market and keeping it there.

I know the reaction you're having right now: "Whoa . . . the same amount as the development effort? My market is different!" Okay, then prove it. A simple exercise is to pull the financials of a publicly traded company in the same market as you, and see what they spend. The numbers will show that between 40 and 60 percent of gross revenue usually goes toward sales and marketing. This typically represents ongoing sales and marketing efforts; a product launch usually takes considerably more. So, start with a budget metric at least equal to your development investment.

The next trap I see companies falling into is not having any money left for a launch and sales and marketing effort once the product is finally built. The simple answer, then, is this: Don't build it. No one will find you, no matter how spectacular your product is. A better alternative is to take your budget, allocate half for the sales and marketing effort, and through Market Validation, develop a product for half the original estimate by focusing your market, reducing your features, and dominating in a smaller market that's easier to get to. Once you've gotten traction there, expand your market with subsequent releases using the same expense allocation guidelines—where the development budget is equal to the first year's sales and marketing effort—to take on additional, tightly targeted markets. Dominate three or four of these submarkets, and you probably have effective control of the superset market.

APPROACH AND LAYOUT OF THIS BOOK

This book integrates a broad range of business skills and activities, combining and applying them in a unique set of ways to analyze markets. It touches a broad range of disciplines, including market research, statistics, data collection, product development, buyer behavior, product launches, project management, sales, marketing, organizational behavior, product life cycles, and countless other topics. In and of themselves, these topics have volumes of books and material written on them. Specialists have built careers studying them.

That said, the goal of this book is not to explain any of these disciplines, which would not make for an interesting book, nor would there be enough space to cover them all adequately. The business world has countless experts, educational sources, books, and firms that can provide detailed guidance in any one of these fields. My goal with this book is not to teach you about these disciplines but to show you how to use them to improve your business. If you would like to dive deeper into any of the subjects covered here, I would invite you to do so by pursuing the details through the appropriate expert.

Readers of my first book, *A Good Hard Kick in the Ass,* will recognize a similar treatment of the major topics. When I cover the topic, I'll discuss it, give you a practical way to implement it, and frequently provide a case-study-style example that covers how a real business implemented that particular effort.

The examples will cut across all industries and company sizes to reinforce that this approach is not specific to the industry or size of your company. As you apply the principles of this book, you are objectively evaluating markets, and the position from which you are doing so is the same for all industries and company sizes.

The nature of examples will be biased a bit toward technology companies. This is because these companies regularly experience disruptive technologies and complete market changes measured in months and quarters versus years for other industries. As an example, there have been few real changes to the technology behind cars (the internal combustion engine) and Coca-Cola (the secret formula gets updated only based on new ingredients being used) over the last century. But if you look at the evolution of a company like Intel, Google, or Boeing, you see product life cycles dramatically compressed. In the laboratory of business, technology companies are like the DNA researcher's fruit flies, and we need to use them to represent some of the concepts.

A small detail I would like to address early is the use of the terms "product" and "services." I will use them interchangeably along with the term "offering" in this text. My definition of a *product* is that it is a tangible, manufactured item, such as a car, a personal computer, a combine, or an electrical generator. My definition of a *service* is that it is an intangible item that provides a benefit, such as a mutual fund, an insurance policy, or the delivery of a package. The approach to performing Market Validation is the same for both; there are, however, some subtle differences with respect to accessing market requirements, which will be covered in the book.

At a top level, this book presents an introduction, which you are currently reading, and then breaks out the three major steps of Market Validation into three main parts: *Ready, Aim,* and *Fire.* Each of these parts can be read independently, but to get the full benefit of the Market Validation process, I suggest reading them sequentially, as they are interdependent.

Ready covers what you need to do to figure out if your idea is worth pursuing. The term "pursuing" can be taken broadly; it could mean anything from investing more of your personal time on the weekends to convincing your current employer to invest in the opportunity or quitting your day job to pursue it. Before you do any of these, go through Part 1 and do all the work required around *Ready.* It can be done with as little as a few days of effort, and before you mortgage that house or raise your hand to volunteer for a new product assignment with your current employer, make sure you've done some of the fundamentals to evaluate if it's an idea with merit.

Once you've graduated from *Ready,* you're onto *Aim. Aim* is where the really diligent work gets done. Whereas *Ready* can potentially be done in a few days, *Aim* requires real effort around reaching out to the market and aggressively gathering data from a number of different sources. This will be explained in detail in the book. In general, you'll need to allocate the majority of the 60 days of effort for Market Validation to get through the *Ready* and *Aim* phases. If you're a scrappy start-up, we'll cover how to reduce the expenses here with elbow grease. If you're a funded company or a new product effort in an established company, we'll go deep on what other sources you can use to speed this process along.

The final step, *Fire,* ultimately is critical, because it is the follow-through on all the work and effort of the first two phases. I will cover in depth how to launch, market, and sell your product using the results of Market Validation, which will ultimately produce better results with less effort based on the work done in the first two phases.

With all the Market Validation projects I've done, I've coined some terminology germane to the process. I've also used some terminology from my first book, *A Good Hard Kick in the Ass,* which touched on the subject. As a reference, I've included this terminology here.

TERMINOLOGY

Aim: The second step of Market Validation, using the metaphor of *Ready, Aim, Fire. Aim* involves investing a significant amount of time and effort in analyzing and understanding first-hand your target market and how to best serve it with a new product or service offering.

Back of the envelope: Interpret this as a loose guideline; something where you can use a generalized rule to approximate an answer. See also **rule of thumb.**

Business person: I'll use this term to refer to a prototypical business person throughout this text. This person could be male or female and have any level of experience or education. The assumptions are that this person is eager and observant, has business knowledge, and is characterized by a desire to pursue a successful offering.

Business pornography: The media covering business have to boil subjects down to small, digestible sound bites to make them interesting. Around new products, this results in the media giving you the impression that launching a new product or service is simple, usually successful, and does not require a lot of effort. In my experience, the exact opposite is true.

Check box items: The tendency for business people to focus on discrete, minor action items versus big picture goals. Businesses like to manage, and to manage infers looking at lots of data, so frequently, these types of activities get confused with real value creation. When dealing with new products, value creation comes from delving deep into external markets instead of analyzing and managing lots of internal data.

Domain knowledge: This refers to an individual's or team's knowledge from working in a particular industry. In general, you want a team launching a new product to have "domain knowledge" in the market category they are entering. See also **execution intelligence.**

Execution intelligence: This refers to the ability of a management to get something done. The idea behind execution intelligence is that no one person is a business superhero, and it takes a team to have the collective ability to get a business off the ground. Also see **domain knowledge.**

Fire: The final step of Market Validation, using the metaphor of *Ready*, *Aim*, *Fire*. This step is where all the data and resources that were gathered and used in the *Ready* and *Aim* process are brought together to build a market-oriented product and effectively launch it into the market.

Market Validation: The process of objectively evaluating the market for your offering and understanding the target market and required features before making the investment to build it and bring it to market.

Output orientation: In the context of launching new products, the general tendency of good business people to work long hours doing things that may not be creating value.

Primary research: Research you conduct directly; for example, going directly to a potential customer and asking them a series of questions. This is in contrast to **secondary research.**

Products, services, and offering: These words are all used interchangeably throughout this text. Regardless of whether you're developing a product or service, you will use the same Market Validation process and framework.

Quantitative: Using numbers versus logic or deduction, typically in an analysis or research context, to make your case.

Qualitative: Using logic or deduction versus numbers as a basis for your analysis.

Ready: The first step of Market Validation, using the metaphor of *Ready, Aim, Fire.* This step is a relatively fast, high-level triage of a market opportunity to gauge whether it is worth investing the time and effort it takes to move through the remaining Market Validation steps.

Research and development: Also abbreviated as "R&D." This refers to the effort of both researching how to build a product and actually building it. In the context of this book, it refers generically to the efforts around building the product. Also see **sales and marketing.**

Rule of thumb: I use this term when providing a guideline versus an absolute way of doing things. Loosely translated, you should interpret this to mean 80 percent of the time. See also **back of the envelope.**

Sales and marketing: Also abbreviated as "S&M." This covers all the sales and marketing efforts. *Marketing* refers to the process of narrowing down leads from the target market to people who are qualified and ready to buy. *Sales* refers to the process of taking people who are ready to buy and selling them the product. *Sales and marketing* together refers to the collective effort of narrowing down a broad universe to the people who actually buy the product. Also see **research and development.**

Secondary research: Research where the interviewing process, data analysis, and conclusions were done by some other source. This is in contrast to **primary research.**

STEP 1

READY—COULD THIS IDEA FLY?

CHAPTER ONE
Ready

The Overview

So you've got an idea stuck in your head. And, like a bad song, it just won't go away. I know the symptoms well. Sound familiar? Then you really, really need to read this section.

This section gives you a relatively quick and objective way to evaluate whether the opportunity you're pursuing is worth taking to the next step. It is designed to be a quick-hitting, back-of-the-envelope process that really represents a market triage—qualifying a market to see if there's enough potential to invest more time and effort. There's nothing fancy here; just a systematic process to figure out if there's enough juice in the market you're interested in to warrant further investment of time and resources. I will say this over and over again, but in my experience success is based on a series of fast failures, and this is the first step in the painful extrusion process of figuring out if you have got a compelling market or if it's time to move on to the next opportunity.

In this section, I'll walk you through the five checklist items of the *Ready* phase of Market Validation. This will give you a way to objectively evaluate the merits of your idea by evaluating the market for it. Some of what you're about to read will seem simple and enlightening. Some of it will be difficult and frustrating. If the market indicators give you a green light to proceed, you'll probably be elated. If the data gives you cause for concern, you'll be frustrated, but in the end the data are objective and your emotions will not be. I am really just trying to isolate your emotions from the decision-making process. Either way, I promise you, once you apply this method, you'll be able to evaluate your idea through the prism of real, objective data. And the way you look at your current idea, and any ideas you have going forward, will never be the same.

In the end, it's your decision to make as to whether your idea is worth pursuing. Keep in mind, this decision can be difficult to make objectively for anyone who is passionate about an opportunity. You must step outside yourself and be intellectually honest about the results. Only then can you decide whether to go on to the next steps outlined in this book, or pursue the next potential market on your list. Remember this mantra: The key to success is fast failures. It's a positive outcome if, after a few days of doing the work in this section, you decide not to pursue the opportunity. I have known many people who have invested many years—not to mention their reputations, houses, and retirement accounts—pursuing things that would have never passed this initial triage process. Doing the work I outline here will ensure you don't make that mistake.

How much time will this take? As little as two days if you have access to the kind of data that's needed. I know how badly people want answers quickly, but the key point at this stage is taking the time to get the right data to make the right decision. The more time you invest, the more certain your conclusions. You must not expect fast, easy answers. I'm getting you at the truth *now*, instead of after you ship, which is when most people discover the reality of what they've built.

If this is a personal project, or if you're contemplating a start-up and don't have a lot of money to put into it, I'll show you how you can substitute time for money in gathering some of this specialized data. If you've got the backing of your current company or others sources of capital, you'll be able to purchase some of the more specialized data and move though the process more quickly.

Again, think of this as the *triage period*—the period during which you make your initial evaluations—of your idea, of the market, of your competition, of how others have evaluated your market. Okay. Let's get started.

CHAPTER TWO

Domain Knowledge

Where Did You Get Your Idea?

New product dreams capture the imagination. They're exciting, motivating, and become all consuming, and they need boundless passion to see them through to market viability. And, all too often, they can lead the dreamer into a venture whose very premise is terribly unrealistic. The result? The dream becomes a nightmare as the product comes crashing down.

EVALUATING YOUR IDEA: WHERE DID IT COME FROM?

How do you start the process and lay a realistic foundation? First, by evaluating the *source* of your idea. Did it come from your work with customers in your job? From your experience as an ordinary consumer? Or from a major event in your consumer life, such as buying a house, having an accident, or some other infrequent, high-impact experience?

It's worth taking a look at each of these possibilities. Why? Because the underlying source of your idea speaks volumes about the potential of your market. What we're digging into is your domain knowledge on the subject by evaluating where the idea originated. This can speak volumes about the opportunity and your ability to effectively pursue it.

JOB EXPERIENCE

Bottom line: Based on my years of Market Validation experience, I can say with confidence that, if your market opportunity is based on your job experience, it is fundamentally the best type of opportunity to pursue. This is assuming you've been in the industry you are pursing for more than 10 years.

This level of job experience brings two positive attributes with it. First, you are 10 years down the learning curve about the industry you are evaluating. You know the trends, the players, the competitors, the customers, the distribution channels, and all the other wisdom it can take years to accumulate. When you're entering a market with a new product in an area you already have experience in, all this information puts you well ahead of people who are entering the market while trying to simultaneously figure out the industry.

The second advantage to sticking with what you know is that it removes the urge to strike out and do something new and different, which is a part of human nature. I'm not against new and interesting experiences, but I am against them when you need to have every advantage you possibly can when entering a new market. Here's the bottom line: You want to have already learned about your market on someone else's nickel.

So those are the pluses of pursuing an opportunity based on job experience. Here's the downside: You know the subject matter *too well*. You tend to rely on instincts and experience to make decisions. And the truth is, you *need* those instincts and experiences—but you need to back them up with outside, objective confirmation.

Any market worth pursuing is changing at a rapid rate, so anything you knew yesterday you have to treat as suspect today. Moreover, if your experience comes from inside one company, it has probably seen success (or you wouldn't be pursuing a similar opportunity or be working there in the first place). That success came from an established offering, and you will now be entering that or a similar market anew. You must get really current, objective market data and not take comfort in the fact that you currently work at a company that was successful in its category.

Let's also cover a closely related topic that should not be misconstrued as domain knowledge. That's seeing an opportunity based on working in the current job you do—seeing an opportunity for a product or service based on how you work or how your company works.

The challenge here is that business people think, because they could use a widget in their day-to-day job, everyone could; or because their company uses a dozen of these same widgets, there must be a big market for them. I'm not saying this isn't true. I'm just saying you must carefully evaluate demand *outside* your immediate work ecosystem to prove that there's a real market opportunity.

Too many times I've seen people get really excited about something that would make their work life easier and go on to extrapolate big market trends based on a couple of data points. When I'm approached about these kinds of opportunities and I ask them my inevitable Market Validation question, people look slightly indignant and say, "Of course I did my Market Validation!" When I probe deeper, this Market Validation involved polling colleagues and friends who have their same views, including work peers, brothers-in-law, and drinking buddies. Be aware, most of your friends will go out of their way to encourage you to "pursue your dreams." Your dream may be a start-up, or an entrepreneurial pursuit at your current employer, and you should expect your friends to be supportive, but that does not qualify them to judge the merits of your potential product. Enjoy their support, but don't rely on it. Instead, use the methods that follow to ensure that you have a real, proven market for your idea. I have seen many talented business people aspiring to enter a new market make massive market projections based on a couple of nonobjective data points. Using this technique in the brutal world of capitalism will put you in the road-kill category pretty quickly.

EXPERIENCE AS A CONSUMER

We work at our jobs to give us the freedom and income to pursue interests outside of work, which makes us pretty good consumers. People who enjoy the game of business look at how often they pull out their wallet to pay for something—at a retail or grocery store, a doctor's office, a gas station, you name it.

We tend to want to figure out if there are faster and more efficient ways to deliver these typically retail products and services that are in the universe of our consumer lives. The problem is, as consumers, we tend to think of ourselves as experts in those products, when in reality we are expert consumers of those products—not expert *producers* of those products. So it's critical to separate domain knowledge based on work experience from experience based on repeat usage of products or services in our consumer lives.

THE LAW OF LARGE NUMBERS

The last point that needs to be made on idea source is the lure of large numbers. Many business professionals aspiring to enter a new market go after what I like to call the "China effect." This means pursuing markets where the numbers are huge. The classic symptoms are to look at markets like China—the grocery business, health care, and residential real estate based on the huge numbers, either in quantity or dollar value, that are associated with these markets.

Here are the things you need to watch out for on these fronts. First and foremost, many people end up pursuing these markets based on nothing more than their size: If I could sell one energy drink to everyone in China, if I could get a 5 percent share of the energy drink market in the US, if I could get my house-closing automation software used by fewer than 1 percent of real estate brokers, if I could get my new herbal remedy for diabetes to be the standard of care in the medical field.

These are all great and noble goals, but the reality is these markets are all controlled in one way or another by huge forces—everything from governments, to established brands, to the atomic nature of local businesses that always buck standardization, to the daunting complexity of the healthcare system. These are noble goals to build a company vision on, but to win in a market with a new product or service, you have to go after a market that has significant market pain, a pervasive problem, and a willingness to pay for a fix. Bottom line, build on your grand vision one market segment at a time.

CHAPTER THREE

The Market

How Big Is It and How Fast Is It Growing?

After you examine the source of your idea and evaluate its validity, it's time to move on to analyzing the industry you're contemplating. What is the size of a market, how fast is it growing, and why do these factors matter? It's imperative that you answer these questions as part of your new venture.

At this, the *Ready* stage, it's okay to do this at a broad level; later, during the *Aim* phase, we'll see how you can do it at the level of market segments and subsegments.

Why determine your market's size and growth rate? Here's why: The size of a market indicates whether it can support a new entrant. And the growth rate predicts whether there's room to maneuver toward success. When you're entering a new market you want every possible advantage on your side, and size and growth rate are some of the easiest ways to figure this out.

SIZE: IS THE MARKET BIG ENOUGH FOR YOUR AMBITIONS?

That's right: The size of the market you need depends on your ambitions for your new product. A major industrial player looking to enter a market for a manufactured good probably needs eventual revenue in the hundreds of millions of dollars to justify the risk and investment needed to design and build a manufacturing facility and develop worldwide distribution. During the triage period, their minimal criteria would require a worldwide market measured in the billions of dollars to support their eventual revenue goal measured in the hundreds of millions of dollars.

For example, a worldwide market size of $10 billion annually would require 1 percent market penetration to support $100 million in annual revenue. A macro, back-of-the-envelope analysis would suggest the market is big enough to support the company's product ambitions. Why? Simple math. Market penetration of 1 percent yields revenue of $100 million.

Alternatively, if the worldwide market size is $1 billion annually, hitting the company's product revenue goals requires 10 percent penetration, a more significant—and more difficult to reach—goal. Other features, such as the life cycle of the segment and the growth rate of the category, factor in here, but we'll look more closely at those later.

On a smaller and more local scale, let's consider an entrepreneur with ambitions to open a series of coffee shops in a major metropolitan area in the United States, an area with a population of 750,000. The entrepreneur has domain expertise based on her current experience as a District Manager for Starbucks, managing 10 shops in the same geography.

From her domain knowledge, she knows that in order to tap into the area she needs a series of stores geographically dispersed based on population density. She also knows that, to be successful, each store has to generate $500,000 of gross revenue a year. Her overall question at this point is, does this opportunity represent something she should invest more time in evaluating?

The first step in figuring this out is to ask: Is the current market opportunity big enough to support another player?

These two companies differ dramatically in size, industry, and business models, but the overall market sizing effort is the same: Figure out the market size, and at a macro level understand what kind of penetration is needed to support the business. Clearly, the more percentage penetration required to support the business, the lower the relative attractiveness of the opportunity.

GROWTH RATE: IS IT HAPPENING IN THIS MARKET?

Ask an intellectually honest entrepreneur or intrapreneur about what made them successful and they'll frequently quote a fair amount of luck: being at the right place, at the right time, with the right product.

Talk to any similarly inclined business person about the success of their business, and they'll tell you a similar story about rapidly rising revenues covering lots of mistakes and making management look really smart.

The point of all this can be summed up in the famous quote, "A rising tide raises all boats." So when you're launching a product, one key thing you want to find is the fastest growing market you can. Strong revenues make it possible to overcome mistakes, and strong revenues are easiest in a faster growing market.

We'll cover more granular details on this as we move forward in this book through the Market Validation steps. For now, here are a few of the bigger points to keep in mind on market growth rate.

Faster growing markets are those with accelerating growth, implying new customer entrants. These are on the "growth" side of the product adoption curve (more on this later). The more new customers, the more opportunity for sales to customers just entering the market. That's always less costly than taking share from a competitor. Industry estimates put the cost of displacing a competitor at 3 to 10 times the cost of acquiring a new customer. So, in its elegant simplicity, a faster growing market is more attractive because of the reduced cost of acquiring customers.

On the flipside, slow growth markets are typically more difficult to enter. These markets are decelerating in growth, which typically represents mature customer usage and high feature and pricing sensitivity.

This slow growth market situation puts the advantage in an incumbent supplier's hands on multiple fronts, including knowledge of the customer base, presence in all aspects of the product infrastructure, and strong domain knowledge. With respect to business categories, any category involving an investment in fixed assets (manufacturing being the prime example) over the long period of time it typically takes for a market to reach maturity implies that established players have strong pricing power based on the full amortization of their equipment. They can drive prices down dramatically long enough to make it impossible for you to stay in the market, because of the new, fixed costs you need to cover. Put another way, they can hold their breath longer than you can.

WHAT TO MEASURE YOUR GROWTH RATE AGAINST

The number to use as a benchmark to compare your segment's growth rate is the overall growth rate of the economy in a similar geography. So if you plan to enter a market with a new product in North America, the growth rate of the overall market (as measured by Gross National Product or Gross Domestic Product) has averaged around 4 percent over the last 10 years. So, ideally the growth rate of the market you are entering here would be well above this number.

Conversely, if you were entering a market with a new product in China, with its higher overall growth rate, you would need a higher growth rate bar to clear to have an equivalent opportunity.

Bottom line, during the triage phase, a market with a growth rate above GNP or GDP in your target geography should be much more valuable than one below.

EVALUATING MARKET SEGMENTS

As we will explore in more detail later, when entering a new market, it's better to target a specific *subcategory* of that market than the broader overarching market category.

The natural tendency when entering a market is to target a large, generalized market with a broad feature set. The product gets designed to reach across the various subsegments of the target market in an effort to go after as big an opportunity as possible.

The reality is, this typically leads to generic products that barely touch on the needs of many submarkets in an effort to be a cure-all for their combined broader market. When a new product is launched using this approach, there is nothing distinctive for any of the market segments, and the product tends to appear mediocre and unfocused. Additionally, since this broad market strategy is driven by an attempt to go after big numbers, the sales and marketing efforts get expensive fast. Not only do we have a watered-down product addressing a too-generic set of requirements, but we also have high expenses around getting the product message out.

The key to addressing this is to take a page from General Electric's handbook during the Jack Welch days. Don't try to go after a broad, generalized market. Assemble all the submarkets of that broader market, carefully analyze those submarkets, and target one of them.

When you go after a narrower market segment, you incorporate fewer features, thereby saving time and money on development. In addition, you more accurately pinpoint your sales and marketing efforts on a focused market, making your sales and marketing more efficient. In the end, delivering a product with a shortened development cycle to an efficiently targeted market leads to more revenue, less expense, and a shorter time to market.

As I discussed in my first book, *A Good Hard Kick in the Ass*, I liken this technique to developing a heat-map of a market; your goal is to figure out where the market opportunity is the highest, making for an easier market entry based on your company's skill sets. You want to understand the broad market size and growth rate, then drill down to each of the submarkets to understand *their* sizes and growth rates. From there, you can research market characteristics that let you prioritize which submarket to tackle first.

For example, each of the segments will have different growth rates. Does it make sense to go after the fastest growth segment? Or is that where anyone with a new product goes to for the same reason? Is there a segment that is smaller but has less competition? Or is it dominated by an incumbent that is taking their eye off the market? Is there an anticipated technology shift that will disrupt certain market segments more than others? Is there a target demographic that has a higher growth rate, or other more attractive characteristics?

Breaking down the overall market into its subsegments enables you to figure out which segment to go after first. You will end up developing a more precise set of features that can be delivered more quickly and that lend themselves to more precise sales and marketing. Do this, combined with the other techniques in this book, and you'll be able to ship the right product sooner, win in your first market, then build on that success and leverage your way into the other submarkets.

The bottom line is this. The big mega-corporations of today that dominate huge markets didn't get there overnight. At some point in their heritage, there was one person with one idea that went after a reasonably bounded market opportunity and won. They took that success and expanded into others. Some new markets worked, some didn't, but in the end they were able to build on each success until they dominated many markets by first dominating the submarkets within those markets.

CHAPTER FOUR

Lifecycles and Trends

How Are These Affecting Your Market?

Market lifecycles are crucial, and you must understand them. The market lifecycle determines the level of growth, not to mention the types of customers in your target industry.

There are many great resources for more material on lifecycles, including books and web sites. For our purposes, I'll provide a high-level overview and describe what matters most during the triage, *Ready,* phase of your Market Validation process.

MARKET LIFECYCLES: WHERE'S YOUR ENTRY POINT?

Market lifecycles are broken into four significant types of buyers, each with their own attributes: early adopters, early majority, late majority, and laggards. From your perspective, each has advantages and disadvantages. And each is served by companies with specific business characteristics.

Early Adopters

You've probably heard this term before, and it's frequently associated with users of technology. You probably know people who always have the newest cell phone, GPS system, or big screen television. These people are the early adopters, and their presence represents a nascent market that could be or is experiencing high growth.

Getting technical, on a normal distribution curve, this is the leading-edge tail that is slowly growing with a slope that's still less than 1.

That last sentence says a lot. If the category has started to get traction in the market, it will grow very quickly. If it hasn't yet gained market traction, it will take considerable investments in cash and time to get it there. Which side of that market traction you are on can make all the difference in the world. The key here is understanding how much prompting (meaning sales and marketing investment) customers need to purchase the product.

At this stage of market development, costs are typically high; the product category is new, volumes are low, and the manufacturing learning curve has had minimal effect on production efficiencies. If you enter a market at this stage, be prepared to dole out plenty on manufacturing and sales and marketing.

That's the bad news about the market. The good news is you will typically have little or no competition. This is, of course, assuming you are *early* into the market and are not using a fast-follower approach to rapidly enter a market someone else has proven.

A final and important point: It is very hard to make money at this point of market development. As highlighted, costs are high for manufacturing and sales and marketing—the two major expense items for any new product or service offering.

The best way to play this type of market is to be a significant market shareholder as the market segues from early adopters to early majority. This transition will bring with it a major reduction in sales and marketing costs, and if you can be one of a very few players at that point in time, you should see significant profitability. Until, of course, some fast followers see what is going on and jump into the pool with you.

Companies at this stage in today's world are frequently technology or life sciences companies. Examples of products in this category on the technology front would be Apple's iPhone, which is still in its early adopter phase (as I write, it has only one cellular carrier in the U.S.), and the pharmaceutical drugs that treat restless leg syndrome (as evidenced by heavy advertising to educate the masses on the fact that the disease exists and has a cure).

The Early Majority

A market enters its early majority phase when end-user demand becomes mainstream. The heavy investment to reach, educate, and close customers in the early adopter lifecycle has been made, and the payoff is increasing overall demand for the product. Sales and marketing investments still need to be made, but not at the furious rate needed for the early adopter stage.

At this stage, products become more mainstream. For example, the corresponding industries achieved early majority status when GPS navigation systems began showing up in cars from the factory, high-definition televisions became available at stores like WalMart, and competitors started flooding the market with products that compete with Apple's iPod. Speaking of which, companies that use a fast-follower strategy typically start entering at this point; classic examples are companies like Dell and Microsoft.

Going back to the technical interpretation, on a normal distribution curve, we're out of the leading-edge tail and climbing the beefy, steep part of the curve that is now growing fast with a slope that's greater than 1. The space under the curve represents the high volume of products being shipped and customers that are in the market.

This is an ideal market now if you're already in it, and you're incredibly well positioned if you have just entered it. You're stepping onto a rocket ship of demand, and you're benefiting from all the investments other companies have made to create that demand. If you're just entering, chances are you're able to use newer and less expensive manufacturing techniques and take advantage of economies of scale that did not exist in the lower volumes of early adopters.

That's the good news. The bad news is, markets are efficient, competitors are aggressive, and capital moves to areas where it gets the most return. Hence, your market is now a target for anyone in adjacent markets, not to mention start-ups. Companies that can move easily into this market will ride the same rocket ship, and existing companies and outside investors will aggressively fund competitors in the space if they are not already in the market.

This increasing number of competitors and decreasing costs will also bring with it a natural decrease in price points as volume increases. In this phase of the product lifecycle, the costs of marketing and production are decreasing more quickly than prices, so profitability is typically pretty good.

If you are already in this market, your strategy is to grow your share at all costs. Keep delivering your product or service as is, making few, if any, feature enhancements or quality improvements. You're embroiled in a land grab for market share and need to aggressively focus on this while the market is hot.

Late Majority

The late majority stage occurs with market saturation, when user demand begins to slow. Sales volumes peak, demand has been more and more fulfilled, and prices drop as competitors enter the market.

Companies in this category respond by emphasizing brand and differentiating with features. Since fewer customers are entering, sales and marketing budgets tend to be focused on grabbing market share from competitors—a much more expensive proposition than getting new customers to consider your brand.

A classic example here would be Coke and Pepsi in the US market. Overseas they are experiencing expanding growth, but in the US this market share is in decline. Tastes have changed, and more juice, sports, and energy drinks have come into the market to compete in the broader drink market. Coke and Pepsi continue to market heavily, but they tend to take each other on directly with claims of taste (typically with new calorie-free sweeteners) or consumer promotions. Their marketing efforts focus on taking share from each other versus capturing new consumers. This reflects flat-to-declining market growth that means your best source of customers use your competitor's brand. This does not make for an easy market for a new entrant to break into.

From a technician's view, demand has peaked, so we are over the mid-point hump of the distribution curve. We are on the downhill side, with demand still growing, but at an ever-decreasing rate, with the slope of the decline being less than -1.

This type of market is not a good one to enter. The many competitors that were drawn in during the early majority stage are feeling the pinch and will readily cut prices to keep profitability up. They also have established channels of distribution and outlets that they can lock up. They have established customer bases that they can communicate with that have demonstrated brand loyalty. Enter with extreme caution.

There is, however, one attractive strategy for new entrants.

That strategy is to enter with a "mid-life kicker" product. Such a product adds some innovation that dramatically increases price-performance. It also sparks an entirely new product lifecycle at the early adopter stage.

Examples here include the current spate of multiple-hour energy drinks entering the soft-drink market, the transition in music delivery from LPs to tape to CDs to MP3 players (keep in mind that you pretty much replace your music collection at one of these shifts), and the addition of the BluRay high-definition format to DVDs.

Mid-life kicker products are common in the pharmaceuticals industry. These products are introduced when the price-performance of a drug is changed, either when patents expire and generic versions flood the market at lower price points, or when over-the-counter availability causes volumes to increase dramatically.

Bottom line: Stick to the mid-life kicker strategy when entering a late majority market with a new product.

Laggards

At the laggard stage, the market is completely saturated, volumes are past their stage of rapid decline and have begun to stabilize, and revenue and profitability are falling. Competitors tend to consolidate to reduce costs and optimize selling and distribution efficiencies. The market is going to stabilize at much lower volumes than the peak, and in some cases simply disappear.

The only real strategy for a company in this phase of the lifecycle is to either sell out to a consolidator or become a consolidator.

Entering this market with a new product that has no significant competitive advantage is suicidal. The remaining competitors have amortized all their fixed costs, leaving mostly the variable costs of manufacturing and distribution. So, short of being able to enter without any fixed costs, it's hard to see this stage of the market lifecycle as a winner for a new entrant.

The only way to consider entering this market is if you have some way of becoming a market dominating consolidator—something almost impossible for a new entrant.

A classic market example of a laggard (it could also be argued as late-majority) lifecycle would be the automobile manufacturing business. There is worldwide oversupply of manufacturers and products, sparking aggressive competition for customers. There is much consolidation as players that are exiting or shrinking sell off some of their brands. What's more, there are no significant technology breakthroughs; consider, for example, that the Ford Model T got about 18 miles per gallon, which is more efficient that the current average for U.S. car makers. As evidenced by recent government bailouts, the U.S. auto industry has been unable to gain share in a market of aggressive competition.

MARKET LIFECYCLES: A SUMMARY

Hopefully, it's now apparent why lifecycles matter when considering which markets to enter with a new product.

Products do well when they are in rapidly expanding markets, and your new product will have a much higher likelihood of success in a growth market. Simply stated, it's much easier to sell your product to a *new* customer than to your competitor's customer.

The back-of-the-envelope method that savvy business people and investors use involves cutting the lifecycle normal distribution curve in half at the peak, and then assessing which half the target market resides in—the first half being the growth segment, and the latter half the decline segment. It isn't always possible to assess a market's lifecycle stage in real time with volume numbers. But you can simply look at growth figures to determine whether it's in the growth phase or the decline phase.

BROAD MARKET TRENDS: HOW DOES YOUR IDEA PLAY?

An important part of triaging your idea during the *Ready* phase is to understand some of the broader economic trends in the market. For now, I am defining these trends as large, macroeconomic trends to consider in the *Ready* stage. You have no control over these factors, but you must understand them in order to adequately evaluate your market.

In previous sections, we evaluated the growth rate of your market and compared this with the overall growth rate of the economy to see where your market falls. We established that you have a higher chance of success in markets that are growing above the average market growth rate in the geography you are competing in. We looked at market lifecycles, noting that opportunities on the growth side of the curve are most likely to succeed.

Now we'll evaluate some of the larger events shaping what's going on in business. For broad coverage, we'll focus on trends in the consumer sector, manufacturing, life sciences, technology, and service-related categories.

CONSUMER SECTOR

On the consumer front, the developed world is clearly the largest buyer of consumer products—products that are called consumables and purchased on a regular basis. North America, Europe, and the Pacific Rim represent the largest markets for these types of products.

Wal-Mart is the largest U.S. company today, with annual revenues of $404 billion dollars. While they have revenue that puts them at the top of the list, their profitability is not as interesting, usually running after-tax between 1 and $1\frac{1}{2}$ percent. That's a whole lot of revenue without a lot of profitability. If you're going to compete in this category, you'll clearly need scale, and you'll need to do this in an industry that has razor-thin margins. How will you be able to pull this off? On the flipside, if you intend to sell through Wal-Mart, how can you make your offer attractive as an upstart product in a category where profits are elusive?

For emerging markets, the global economy has lifted some standards of living, and widespread proliferation of the Internet and satellite TV has upped product demand. It's not unusual to see a peasant in China with a cell phone, or a Masai tribesman in Africa with an iPod. Are these trends your new product is counting on? If so, how will you take advantage of them? Given the knowledge of these trends is fairly widespread, how can you exploit them in ways others can't?

MANUFACTURING

Manufacturing is changing worldwide, as the global economy sees significant increases in transportation infrastructure and the emergence of large population economies like India and China with low labor costs and less stringent environmental standards.

Today, it is not unusual for U.S. companies to ship CAD drawings off to a Chinese or Indian manufacturer to be built. Frequently, the cost of raw materials in the United States equals the cost of finished goods from China, with the only difference being the 30 to 60 day trans-Pacific shipping lag. This has significant implications for Manufacturing in both countries.

At the same time, the United States is still the largest manufacturer in the world, although its volume is declining. Less sophisticated products are built in lower-cost countries with less stringent environmental and safety laws, while the United States dominates in advanced manufacturing.

The trend we are seeing is a migration of manufacturing to areas where labor costs are low, environmental protection is relaxed, and transportation is strong. If you look at these trends you can understand why coastal China has emerged as a worldwide Manufacturing center.

The big unknown, as of the writing of this book, is the impact of the bankruptcy and government bailouts of Chrysler and GM. The automobile industry suffers from worldwide overcapacity, and these vendors have been trounced due to a lack of innovation in their product offerings. It remains to be seen what the longer-term impact of these events will be on the U.S. Manufacturing sector. Clearly, though, if your product uses this sector as a market for your offering, or sells into this sector, you should have a definitive position on where the sector is heading and why you will win—which will be a tough sell given current conditions.

LIFE SCIENCES

Life Sciences products, or medically related products and services, are seeing a large uptick in demand, particularly from developing countries. In these developing countries, the baby boom is nearing retirement age in excellent health and with significant wealth compared to previous generations. Their expectation of continued health is high. Two pieces of evidence confirm this: the significant number of advertisements seen regularly for age-related diseases, and the preponderance of cancer, heart attack, and serious surgery survivors, people who have had Lasik or heart surgery, and recipients of hip or knee replacements.

This points to significant opportunities, but they must be carefully evaluated. Demand for pharmaceuticals, medical devices, and medical services in general will go up steadily as the baby boom generation continues to age with the same high expectations for health care. But to adequately service this complex market, you need to know what portion of the market you are going after and what the economics of that segment are. Remember, you do not want to be lured by the "Law of Large Numbers."

What market you are going after can make a significant difference. Within North America, Canada has socialized health care and the United States is privatized. This means in Canada the ultimate customer is the government and in the United States it is the insurance company. So if you're developing a product or service delivered to the medical field, these decision makers have to be included. In the end, doctors and consumers, whom most people assume are the targets for Life Sciences offerings, have minimal impact on the market. The people who are paying for the product have inordinate say on what gets used.

If you're aiming to market a pharmaceutical or medical device, you will need to contend with the U.S. equivalent of the Food and Drug Administration in whatever country you are targeting. In the United States this is an exceedingly long, demanding, and expensive process that must be done if you want to get your product on the market.

One word of caution here on the FDA approval cycles: In the thousands of plans I've seen that require FDA approval, 95 percent of them say they will get on the FDA fast-track based on predicate devices or pharmaceutical offerings. No investor will believe this, because the FDA uses the fast-track approval process on less than five percent of products.

TECHNOLOGY

Technology is probably one of the sexiest fields today. It and Life Sciences tend to attract the largest amounts of venture capital, based on these categories' consistently high market growth rates and the typical company's growth rate and profitability. The challenge of fast-growth, high-profitability businesses is they sometimes have to expand so fast they run out of cash; this is where venture capital typically steps in and fills the void. This only reinforces the importance of market growth rates.

That said, since around the turn of the century, the overall growth rate of the Technology field has slowed from its blistering pace. This, coupled with rampant consolidation, suggests a maturing growth rate in this category. This is significant when you also factor in the product lifecycle impact. Finally, much less venture capital is available for this category than in years past, along with a reduced return of venture investments made in these markets—further suggesting that the category is maturing.

That's not to say Technology markets lack potential; they are arguably some of the strongest in the world. It is simply important, when entering a Technology market with a new product, to be able to articulate how these trends will affect your market and what the company will do to address them.

SERVICES

The Services category is typically fastest growing in developed countries and currently represents 70 percent of the U.S. economy. It is a highly prized category, as it typically relies on intellectual capital, requires no manufacturing, is easy to enter, does not have direct environmental impact, and is growing at a rapid rate. It also tends to produce cash flow quickly and, because the assets are minimal, does not require much capital to enter.

Given that the category requires a minimal cash outlay, it is not only easy to enter but likely to spawn competitors quickly as well. It also tends not to be particularly scalable; that is, if you want to double your revenue, you have to double your headcount.

For these reasons, entering the Services market presents a double-edge sword: minimal capital to get into, but easy for competitors to do the same thing. In addition, a services-oriented company has minimal operating leverage because of its limited scalability, so it is difficult to attract outside investors, as the investment returns will typically not be high.

BUYING PATTERNS

An important big-picture trend that must be addressed is the current buying pattern of the market you are entering. Who are the buyers? What are their concerns? What overall trends are driving buying patterns? You must answer these questions during the *Ready* phase of your Market Validation process.

For example, as I write, in the Consumer market there has been a worldwide slowdown in spending. This is the first time in many years that consumers have started the downward spiral of a recession. A slowing economy and increasing unemployment have contributed, exacerbated by the tightening of consumer credit. In the United States, consumer spending drives about 70 percent of the economy, so you need to understand what effect this will have on your product. Chances are, if you're not selling to consumers, you are selling to someone who does, so understand the supply chain in your chosen market and where consumers sit in it.

On the consumer front, it is important to understand the effect on spending for Life Science products. Beyond consumer-oriented nondurable life science purchases (over-the-counter medications, ice packs, and so on) consumers ultimately don't have much control over how their health care dollars are spent. Insurance companies do. Although we are bombarded with advertisements for pharmaceuticals, all a consumer can do is ask their health care provider about them. Ultimately, a doctor needs to write a prescription, and in most cases a health care plan has to provide reimbursement for that prescription. So don't confuse lots of media pointed at consumers with believing they are they ultimate buyers of these products.

Business buying has also been curtailed, in part by the downturn in consumer spending, and in part by the lack of credit that has affected businesses and consumers alike. If businesses can no longer get credit at reasonable rates, they slow down their spending. In addition to this, all of the new-product companies I work with find themselves with a new buyer on the scene when selling to corporations, and that new buyer is the Chief Financial Officer. Remember, his or her responsibility is to make sure the company is efficiently spending one of its most precious assets—its cash—so expect to have plenty of time with the CFO before closing a deal in the current environment. You must be able to present a strong business case to this individual; the natural thing for a CFO to do is simply keep their money.

In short, the current trend is recession-oriented buying. How will you address this type of environment when launching your new product? Do you expect to still be in a recession? Do you expect it to be over? If you expect it to be over, what evidence do you have it will be? As of the writing of this book, the recession was supposed to be over two quarters ago, and we're still in the middle of it (at least I hope we've progressed to the middle of it!).

One of the best ways I've found to address these issues is to understand where your product lies in your target audience's list of priorities. Simple questions—for example, "Is this a must-have or a nice-to-have?"—can go a long way toward figuring these out. Must-haves (food, medical services, education, transportation) will at least get consideration in hard times. Nice-to-haves will be put off until times are better.

First, find out which of these categories you are in: nice-to-have or gotta-have. Second, where are you on the list of things that need to get fixed now? Top 3? Top 10? If you don't know, you need to pick up the phone and find out. But more of that in the next section: *Aim*.

A strong trend occurring in today's market is the substitution of services for capital purchases. As an example, both consumers and businesses are spending more to repair machinery, cars, and appliances than to replace them. Using some of the criteria we've covered, for most businesses and consumers, things like cars, trucks, and washers and dryers are "must-haves." However, if they break down in this environment, most likely the first option is fixing, not replacing. You need to understand how this substitution of services for a product will affect your offering.

This is also a good example of why thorough substitute analysis (coming up) needs to be done. It's interesting when you consider a mechanic to be a substitute for a new truck, but knowledge of this type of thing is what needs to be second nature to you as you prepare to enter your market.

SOURCES OF CAPITAL

The availability of capital is critical, especially given the current worldwide economic situation. Needless to say, this will affect your new entry on multiple fronts; it could impact whether you get the capital to develop and launch your new product, and it could affect your target market and its access to capital to purchase your product.

Capital in this case is a generic term for the money needed to develop or purchase a product or service. Many times, businesses and consumers will pay cash, particularly for frequent purchases or products with short lifecycles. Other times, consumers and businesses will have access to money in the form of credit, or debt, representing borrowed money that needs to be paid back. Businesses also have access to equity, which represents the cash they generate when they sell stock. Since they have sold a tangible piece of the company, it does not have to be paid back over time but represents an ownership and control interest on the company.

First you need to know how your purchaser will pay for your product or service offering. For example, both businesses and consumers will frequently purchase cars with debt. Why is this? It is an expensive asset, a durable good, with a life expectancy of several years. If it provides value over several years, it makes sense to pay for it over several years. Businesses use this concept broadly; if the company generates profits that exceed its cost of borrowing on a percentage basis, it will typically borrow for large purchases as, even with debt, these purchases have an accretive effect on earnings.

If your business customer will not pay cash, how will they pay for it? Debt? Equity? If they need access to debt or equity markets, will this prolong your selling cycle? Will you need to involve the debt or equity holder in the selling process? Do you need to lay out economic rationale of your product early in the sales process? Do you need to provide financing sources for your offering?

The best illustration of this can be seen in the current bankruptcy of the U.S. car producers GM and Chrysler. They were hit with a double punch. First, the recession caused consumers to curtail their new car buying; then, the credit crisis prevented the few consumers who were interested in new cars from accessing the credit to purchase them.

So, it is critical to understand how your purchaser pays for your product or service.

You must also know how your new product development, launch, and first year of sales and marketing efforts will be financed. Options include bootstrapping, income from other current products or services, debt, equity, and internal capital transfers. Some of these depend on whether you are operating within an established business or starting a new company.

The most straightforward case is bootstrapping or income from other products or offerings. This means you are siphoning off money from a successful product or service to fund a new one. Bootstrapping requires you to get a handle on the reliability of the income stream for those products. You must also develop contingency plans for the new offering if that income is not what you expect.

If you're financing with debt, it probably comes from within an existing operation or something with an asset that can collateralize the debt. Are the terms of the debt currently known? Has the capital been procured, or is it expected in the future? What range of terms is both acceptable and able to produce an accretive product offering?

The same scenario holds true for equity. Is the source of equity for the funding from within the company? Is the company publicly traded? Or is the company private, with equity raised from private sources? Is this the first product offering? Are the terms of the equity offering known? Has the capital been accessed yet? At what price does it need to be available for the project to go forward?

Internal capital transfer funding brings up similar issues. An internally funded project implies that a certain return hurdle rate will need to be met. What is that rate? Does it change, or is it fixed? Is it transferring cash that the company already has, or does it rely on a future event?

POPULATION TRENDS

Population trends affect your market in major ways. You must understand these trends—and have a plan in place for addressing them.

By population, I'm referring to both human and business populations. Both shift frequently, and these shifts are well tracked. Some of the key business population trends were covered in our discussions of Consumer, Manufacturing, Life Science,

Technology, and Service-oriented business categories. Now, let's take a look at human population trends.

As we've discussed, one major population trend is the aging baby boom population in developed countries. Similar trends include the declining populations of these same developed countries, expanding populations in the developing world, as evidenced by China and India, and the emergence of a middle class in these developing countries. This worldwide middle class is beginning to exercise its economic status by buying more consumer products.

Another significant trend is the reduced number of immigrants the United States gives entry to, causing reverse immigration. Now it is not unusual for the best and brightest to come from around the world to the United States for an education, only to return to their home countries and start businesses servicing the United States, such as call centers and manufacturing plants, or serving their own local markets.

Within the United States, populations have moved out of cities and into suburbs around major urban areas. Recent trends, however, show populations shifting back to urban areas, giving rise to major changes in industries such as construction and health care.

Another trend that can be traced to population and demographics is that, over the last several decades in the United States, we have seen an increase in the number of meals eaten outside the house and a dramatic increase in fast food retail establishments. The results are not only an expansion in restaurant offerings, but a shift in grocery store purchases and health care issues.

Other U.S. trends that could affect your business include the population shift away from the industrialized snow-belt cities of the north to southern sunbelt cities, increases in the population with college educations, increases in home ownership, and the shrinking impact of traditional broadcast media as social networking and online advertising become mainstream.

TECHNOLOGY TRENDS

The final big-picture market trend you must consider during the *Ready* phase is the impact of technology on the overall market, along with specific changes it will cause in your market. As a guy who's helped a lot of companies with new products, and invested in a lot of start-up launches, I can tell you that I believe the best market opportunities involve technology that causes disruptions in existing markets. This is when savvy new products can jump in and steal the show while the established players are still trying to figure out what's going on.

A few trends have been alluded to, but let me take some more time to cover their impact.

One of the most current and dramatic is the fall of broadcast media; by "broadcast," I refer to media that produce a one-to-many transfer of information, including television, newspapers, magazines, billboards, and radio. The trend has been talked about for several decades, but in the last several years we have seen an accelerated shift away from broadcast media.

Although many issues can be pointed for the cause of the decline, let me offer one perspective. The goal here is to illustrate how technology can affect a market, how you need to understand this effect on your market, and how this type of disruption creates opportunity.

The main issue with broadcast media is the difficulty in measuring its effectiveness. Advertising in these media is expensive, and the ultimate results can only be guessed at; there is no precise way to measure results.

Enter a number of technologies that did not intend to exacerbate broadcast's fall, but they started by simply providing a more measureable way to understand the effectiveness of advertisements and other marketing efforts.

What are some of the things that have exacerbated the fall? In the parlance of the *Ready* phase, these would be competitors or substitutes. Content delivery has been radically altered by the web. Specialized web sites, fast reporting, blogs, radio over the Internet, digital cameras and recording devices, and countless other innovations have turned ordinary people into potential reporters. Thanks to technology, content is no longer the specialized purview of large reporting organizations, and people with specialized, nonmainstream interests can now be accommodated.

Looking at the other side of this equation, when consumers are given a choice, they typically opt out of advertising-based broadcast media models. The rise of premium cable television, satellite radio, and fast-forward buttons on DVRs gives consumers options they prefer and readily exercise. Add to that services like Google's Adsense that can precision-target messages and directly measure responses, and you can see some of the root causes of broadcast media's fall.

My goal here is to drive home two points. The first is the need to understand the impact of technology on your target market. A few years ago, Google was a search engine, not a threat to broadcast media. In true disruptive style, it has significantly changed the broadcast media world. The second is the need to do thorough and aggressive competitive and substitute analysis (covered in the next section) as part of the *Ready* phase. If you were doing this for either search engines or broadcast media several years ago, this trend would have shown some early signs of emergence.

CHAPTER FIVE

Your Competitors

What Are They Doing?

One of your most valuable sources of information, particularly in the triage phase when you're figuring out if you should proceed further, is competitive analysis. For a variety of reasons, most people don't take it too seriously, and that's a big mistake.

ANALYZING YOUR COMPETITORS: YOUR MOST VALUABLE TOOL

Competitive analysis is absolutely critical for any new business undertaking. A key aspect of competitive analysis is *substitute analysis*. I will cover these (competitive and substitute analysis) separately, because they involve different techniques. However, it's important to point out that I consider any substitute for a product to be its competitor.

Before we dive into this material, I want to bring up, again, the most ubiquitous, consistent, worldwide competitor. This competitor is the same across all industry segments, company sizes, and product or service offerings. What competition is it? "I want to keep my money." To address it, I've included in this section a discussion of economic analysis. A customer wanting to keep his or her money is both a substitute *and* a competitor. In my experience, people launching new products consistently underestimate its power in the customer decision-making process.

COMPETITIVE ANALYSIS

Competition gives you positive validation about your potential offering. It's also a rich source of information. If someone else has a product in the market, and you're entering it, what more can you ask for than a totally exposed target to shoot for? For these reasons, competition needs to be treated as a net positive—and not as a threat. Remember, your competitor is exposed at this point, not you.

The mere fact that one or many competitors are operating in the market proves that an opportunity exists. You should take full advantage of their presence. Analyze everything about them. Remember, too, that from a product lifecycle standpoint, there are stages when entering a market can be very lucrative; the state of your competitor's product lifecycle can have a dramatic affect on your decision to proceed or not.

Knowing another company's product, features, and customers—not to mention how that company researched, developed, funded, and marketed its product—is an effective and efficient way to better understand a market. The bottom line is this: They are in the market today, with a product, getting money from your target audience; why not do everything possible to go through what they have experienced? Doing so can only help you understand your market.

Competitive analysis requires getting completely inside the head of your competitors and understanding everything about them. It's critical to do it *now*—before you get beyond the *Ready* stage.

A simple way to start is a thorough evaluation of their web site. How is their product positioned? What are the key features? Who are they targeting? Do they advertise price? Success stories? Videos? Reference customers? Do they talk about price, quality, or service? Do they offer competitive profiles? How do they market? Sell?

A thorough analysis of their product is the first step. Understand what their strongest features are and who they consider their current competitors.

Next, move to customer references—or, even more valuable, success stories posted on their web site. What are the types of success stories? Do they match up with the product analysis you just did?

Can you buy their product to do your competitive analysis? Do they have evaluation units? Do they let you use products before buying them? If the product is too big or expensive to evaluate in person, they will typically have other material for potential customers to get familiar with the offering. What form does this take? Contact the sales people and do some mystery shopping.

Look at the section on their management team, board of directors, financial backers, or anything else related to corporate structure. Are they a private or public company? If public, they will have annual and quarterly filings available. If private, are they venture-backed? By whom? Who are their board members?

How do they get their product to market? What distributors do they use? Sales channels? Do they sell through retail? What outlets? Go to those outlets and ask the clerks what they know about the product. Do they use distributors? Go talk to them.

Are they a division of a larger company? What can you learn about the larger company? Were they acquired by the current company? If they were, and the acquiring company was public, under many circumstances they will have had to provide significant disclosure on the pre-acquisition condition of the acquired company.

Who are their suppliers? What raw materials are sourced from what suppliers? What are their suppliers' opinions of them?

If they are a private company, public filings might well be available. Most companies, regardless of size, have credit reports accessible from sources like Dunn & Bradstreet and Hoovers. Check these out. More details on getting outside information on them will be covered in Parts 2 and 3, *Aim* and *Fire*.

Here are the caveats on competitive analysis. I've seen many a strong team fall victim to these well-known rat holes. Believe me, they can trip you up.

First and foremost is the tendency to be condescending toward the competitor company, the management team, and the quality of the products. Competitive bluster can be good, even necessary to get ahead, but now is not the time to exercise it. As I said, the bottom line is, they are in the market today with a product, getting money from your target audience, so soak up everything you can. Learn from them so you can beat them when you get to market. Given their position, treat them with nothing but respect. Once you're in the market and beating them it may be time for some trash talking, but wait until you've earned that right. Otherwise you risk this becoming a cultural attribute, something thrown around as a lazy response to all things competitor based.

The next big thing to watch out for is the viability of features and their importance to the customer base, as well as customer loyalty to the installed products. In my experience, most new entrants feel that a simple increase in features of 25 percent or more will somehow cause customers to dump their current products and flock to new ones. This is seldom the case. Usually, when entering a market and taking share from a competitor, head-butting on features is a losing proposition; you need to get the market and the customers to rethink what the problem is that they're solving—with a bias toward your offering.

The other watch-out-for on the competitor front is the tendency to underestimate customer loyalty. Again, companies entering markets often disparage the competition, and if this becomes a cultural attribute it can cause organizational hubris.

Ultimately, customer loyalty itself might be scoffed at, based on the fact that it has been so long denigrated. In my experience, the best strategy is—again—to hold competitors in high esteem until you have earned the right to feel differently. And that right accrues only from your market performance against them.

SUBSTITUTE ANALYSIS

Substitute analysis is a form of competitive analysis. As you evaluate your market, you must dive deeply enough to understand what your customers see as viable substitutes for the competitors' products.

As we saw in the section on business trends, customers often substitute services in lieu of capital purchases for capital-intensive equipment. For example, in the current economic downturn, many consumers and businesses are spending more money maintaining cars and trucks than buying new ones.

One company I worked with in the past was validating the market for software that managed the hiring process. As they validated the market opportunity, they found more substitutes than direct competitors for their software implementation. Some of the major substitutes included homegrown automation systems, outsourcing of the process to recruiting firms, and use of internal staff or departments. They even found one company that had an elaborate physical mail system that competed with their offering. Betty the mail clerk would catch mail going to a particular department, knowing it was a resume based on the address. She would then attach the appropriate inter-office mail distribution sheet to ensure that the resume was circulated to the appropriate hiring managers using the inter-office mail system. All of this would not have been uncovered without a thorough substitute analysis. And needless to say, 5 percent of the paid time of Betty, who was already on the payroll, was a tough price point to beat.

These lines of analysis led to more interesting data as the company analyzed these substitutes with the thoroughness of direct competitors. Some of the substitutes were used because they were variable expenses contingent on performance—meaning that customers paid for the services only as results were delivered, versus making constant fixed payments that would come with an automated system. The customers who used this substitute did so even if the volume of activity was high; they simply found that paying variably only when performance merited it was a better system for them than installing an automated system that carried constant fixed costs regardless of performance.

The company also learned that human resources departments, who were the target market and the formal buyers of the system, did not actually pay for the product; the hiring departments did. This led the company to include major hiring departments as part of the sales process, along with the human resources departments. They also learned that the major hiring organizations, typically sales and manufacturing, liked the results-based expense model of outside contingency service providers, as these departments had budgets for services but not the capital expenditures required for automation purchases. This led the company to offer its product on a monthly billing basis, versus requiring a one-time capital expenditure.

Keep in mind: It was only through a thorough competitive and substitute analysis that this company learned what it did, and all during the early *Ready* phase. Most companies wouldn't have figured out these details until they crashed into the brick walls outlined above after their product was in the market. Think how much time, effort, and money you can save with a thorough competitive analysis in the *Ready* phase.

ECONOMIC ANALYSIS

The last part of competitive analysis involves economic analysis. I categorize this as competitive analysis because, when you sell to businesses, economic analysis is usually part of the competitive analysis process.

As an example, most companies produce profits above their cost of capital. Therefore, investments that produce a return at or above their profit level have the potential to be accretive to the company, or basically increase profits above their current level on a percentage basis. These investments produce more profit than they consume. But don't get too excited yet. Company buying decisions are not this straightforward. You need to understand what those buying decisions are in the market you are targeting.

Most entrepreneurs and intrapreneurs involved with new product development tend to dramatically underestimate the economic return needed for businesses to consider making a purchase decision. The number I see most people with new products lock onto is 30 percent; if they can show a return on investment to the company of 30 percent per year or more on the cost of the product, surely the customer will buy! So goes the thinking. The company selling the new product then constructs an economic analysis spreadsheet. All the potential customer has to do is plug in a couple of costs and labor numbers, hit the calc key, and presto—economic analysis.

On the customer side, the reality is radically different. Lots of investments in a company's business, taken in isolation, can show returns of 30 percent or greater fairly easily. The issue arises from taking the investment in isolation, without understanding the bigger picture of how the business works. So the reality of a 30 percent ROI on the part of a company *selling* a product is nowhere near that in the context of the company *buying* the product.

Beyond looking at the ROI in isolation, most companies trying to sell on ROI also factor in labor costs in their calculations. The thinking is a certain amount of time will be saved in labor, either hourly or salaried. But here's the kicker: Every customer I know does *not* regard labor costs as automatically saved. In the case of hourly labor, the labor cost does not simply disappear; it just shows up in some other part of the operation. In the case of salaried labor, since it is not charged hourly, incremental labor hours are regarded as essentially free since they do not involve overtime pay.

Given these complexities, how does one sell on economics? Frankly, most companies I have worked with have a hard time using this as a key selling point—even companies with the potential to generate economic returns of as high as 200 to 300 percent, or two to three times the original investment. It can work well—if the analysis is credible, understood, and believed by the customer—as a way for the customer to qualify the product as something to investigate, but seldom have I seen it successfully used to really *sell* the product. Ultimately, companies have their own forms of economic analysis that they need to play out, resulting in the economic analysis approach being most effective in the interest-generating phase.

Let's cover some current examples to look at how economic analysis can factor in customers' buying decisions.

Alternative energy is an extremely timely product category that can drive these economic analysis points home. Today, both businesses and consumers are faced with myriad options for energy alternatives. Have you ever noticed how these are seldom sold on straight-up economic analysis? Everything from cars to windmill generators to solar panels is available today, but is typically marketed not around economics, but reduced environmental impact, reduced carbon emissions, or other green-related attributes.

Why? Because, from a pure economics view, nothing beats the energy output of a barrel of oil. There are many other ways to position around oil as an energy source, mostly by emphasizing reduced environmental impact, but the hard-core economic, money-saving returns are simply not there. So why do these noneconomically viable energy alternatives sell? For the same reason companies don't buy purely on economics—sometimes economics are part of the decision, and sometimes other factors outweigh them.

On the flipside, if an energy source were available that had two to three times the energy output of oil, with the identical environmental impact as oil, it would certainly be closely examined. That kind of efficiency increase would cause companies to evaluate the alternative as the economic savings justify investigation; again, that's not the ultimate decision driver, but a factor in the customer screening process.

While we're on the subject of energy, one off-topic note for anyone analyzing alternative energy offerings as potentially new products: One of the unsystematic risks around building successful product offerings in this category is the wild card of government intervention. Overnight, government policies can make one alternative energy source a winner, and another a dog, as differing policies around the world try to jump-start this industry. This is one of the reasons venture capital has been slow to fund offerings in this space; ultimately, success will not be measured in a free market by economic returns, but by a mercurial incentive system driven by outside non market-based policy forces. So be aware of this big-picture issue when pursuing this market.

CHAPTER SIX
The Experts
What Do They Say?

What is one of the best ways for your new product to gain credibility? What's the best way to stay objective during your *Ready* phase? By using a respected outsider's analysis of your potential markets.

OTHER PEOPLE'S DATA: A TOOL FOR SIZING UP YOUR OPPORTUNITY

Having somebody else state your case for you is absolutely invaluable. Not only does it enable you to use objective numbers to make your argument, but you can also get relatively quick access to numbers you'll need if you pursue your market opportunity beyond the *Ready* stage. This section gives you a variety of ways to do this—both for established markets that are tracked, and for nonestablished or emerging markets that are not on anyone's radar screen yet.

SECONDARY MARKET RESEARCH

The term "secondary market research" simply refers to work undertaken by others. When a market is large, or for other reasons attractive enough that companies are thinking about entering it, secondary market research firms step in and analyze the market's trends and attributes. They then sell this information to interested parties.

The presence of these secondary market research firms speaks volumes about the markets they are tracking. The market has to be big enough to attract these firms, who feel they can take the risk of conducting the research and have a ready market of organizations willing to purchase the results.

Some secondary market research firms are household names, like JD Powers for the automotive industry and Nielsen for advertising research. These names have worked their way into the lexicon of ordinary consumers through their use of surveys to rate products. Essentially, these organizations, and others like them, provide the same type of information and data on a commercial basis for people like you who are thinking about entering these markets. All major industries have them, and you need to know who they are, both the names of the firms and the individual analysts who specialize in your market.

A critical point to keep in mind is that you should use secondary market research as a foundation for additional work. Since the data, information, and firm's interpretation are available to anyone with enough money to purchase them, you need to treat them for what they are: material that can be accessed by anyone with enough money to buy the reports. It is not sufficient for constructing your competitive advantage, or certainly for building your product. It is, however, an important resource for understanding some of the larger characteristics of the market.

Let's examine secondary market research firms through a Market Validation lens. First, this type of research implies a large and robust market with companies operating within it. Second, it suggests that there are a reasonable number of other firms following the market or considering entering it.

The presence of these research firms also suggests an established market in terms of product lifecycles. Most market research firms will wait for the early majority before jumping in and studying a market. There are also some firms, particularly in the fast-growing Technology and Life Sciences fields, that pursue promising markets in the early adopter stage.

I know that many of you reading this are using shoestring budgets to work through the processes presented in this book. Some of you are investing nights and weekends pursuing your start-up dreams while keeping your current day jobs. Others have burned the boats and taken the entrepreneurial plunge and are working in very cash-constrained environments. In the following sections, as I outline more details on secondary market research, I also give you some techniques I've found to get some of this data by investing your time, not your money.

WHAT IF THERE'S NO DATA?

At this point in the *Ready* stage, you might find that you're pursuing a market that has yet to emerge, or one that is simply not big enough, or dynamic enough, to have attracted market research firms.

Your challenge? Use the principles in this section to get someone credible to size your potential market. In this case we'll need to use credible sources to come up with data using the broad market trends discussed earlier, and then use the data, along with some business judgment, to extrapolate the new market opportunity. In essence you are being your own analyst for the emerging category, and to maintain objectivity and credibility you are basing your projections on data sources indirectly related to the new category.

An example I'd like to introduce here involves the development of Apple's iPod. Caveat: My portrayal of the iPod development is pure conjecture; I set forth how Apple *could* have done it, using the Market Validation techniques in this book.

Let's paint the iPod scenario. Apple is going through the *Ready* stage of a new product theory it has. The product is the iPod, and we are performing part of the *Ready* process before the world knew what an iPod was. We will build on this example in the coming sections.

First of all, data from credible market research firms could have formed the base case for the iPod market size. The category of the iPod, before it became its own category, was portable music. Portable music started with the advent of the portable radio, which gave way to car radios, boom boxes, the cassette, and CD-based Walkman-type devices. Data for all of these products could be found publicly from numerous market studies and privately from market research firms. Getting the data and combining market penetration statistics with population data from census records covering the relevant time spans would yield a picture of units sold and market penetration achieved. The data could be assembled on a worldwide basis. So, as a start, we've got a set of base cases that showed penetration of these devices as a percentage of the population. We can look at how these products were adopted, how fast their penetration was, and, based on the slope of current demand, where they are in their product lifecycles.

The next source of data we could track is the penetration of the MP file format, which was the most popular music file format before the iPod. In fact, the MP file format was originally used for voice dictation equipment before it became robust enough to handle music. Tracking the use of this file format also could provide an indication of market size for the iPod using some of the same techniques just covered. Tracking MP3 penetration over time would give us more indicators of adoption, units sold, and lifecycle of the technology. We could also track the adoptions of the MP1 and MP2 to see what the adoption curves looked like and get a feel for how quickly the technology was assimilated.

So, as we were doing our *Ready* process for the iPod, we would be able to do market sizing and growth rates basing our analysis on data from credible market research firms using our own extrapolated projections. The key point is we used outside data, combined with census data, to arrive at our market size and growth rate projections for the iPod. Notice we've also increased the credibility of our projections by using data from several different product categories and multiple secondary sources.

REPORTS: GET YOUR HANDS ON ONE

Obviously, you need to access any available reports that are relevant to your space. The fastest and most efficient way is through an existing subscription your company might have or a direct purchase of the report from the analyst firm. If you are part of a large organization contemplating new markets, you most likely have some sort of subscription with some of the relevant firms. Contact your business library and find out who they are.

If the report you need is not available through an existing subscription relationship, contact the firm directly. It's easy to search these firms and peruse summaries of the reports online. Depending on the price of a report, it's not unusual for firms to provide things like tables of contents, tables of figures, executive summaries, and other overviews for review before purchasing. Sometimes, these high-level summaries are sufficient during the *Ready* phase.

For those of you who are budget constrained, you have a few more options. The first is to make sure your Rolodex of friends at big companies with large business libraries is current, and your relationships with these friends is up to date. I've heard that leaving the name of a specific report that a big company has access to lying around, along with your email address, sometimes causes the report to appear anonymously.

Another approach I've used that works well is finding the report, calling the analyst who wrote it, explaining what you're

doing, and letting them know that price is a big issue. I've frequently been able to get my hands on slightly dated reports
covering the same topics; these might be a generation or two
old, but they often contain the kind of data and insight I need.
Another advantage to contacting the analyst is that you can begin
to establish a relationship with him or her, and, as you will see
in later sections, this can be invaluable.

A frequent technique for getting point data (the size and
growth rate of a market and nothing more) is to follow business publications and search for market analysts' quotes. Market
research firms strive to gain credibility and will frequently be
quoted in business publications. Internet and magazine site
searches are the most efficient way to access these numbers.

Finally, you can often access relevant reports at a university
library. What's more, there are often free trial subscriptions available from services like Hoover's and Dun & Bradstreet. If you
are enterprising and tireless in pursuing all the possibilities, you
can likely succeed in obtaining the material you need.

ACCESSING THE ANALYSTS

As I suggested in the previous section, it's imperative that you
contact the analyst and begin to establish a relationship. As you
approach the task of making some tough calls in your pursuit
of a market, it will be extremely useful to have enough of a
relationship with an analyst that you can bounce ideas around.

Frequently, analysts are former industry players and have
tremendous insight into what is going on. It is their job to know
all the players in their coverage areas; in particular, they must
be knowledgeable about potential new entrants. In general, if
you are constructive when dealing with them, and if you show
insight and perspective into the markets they cover, they will be
motivated to build a relationship with you as you develop your
offering.

You should establish relations with these analysts early in
the process—and share your product plans with them if you

end up pursuing the market. They frequently deal in nondisclosure agreements and will be comfortable critiquing your plans without disclosing them to outsiders. As you will see in the section on Quality Influencers, keeping these analysts in the loop as you develop your product can be of tremendous benefit on multiple fronts. First of all, all analysts appreciate a market-driven approach, and sometimes they'll help guide you with their knowledge of the market space. In the end, they will have opinions on your product, and your goal is to get them on board with your market-driven approach. Market data are objective data, and this is their stock and trade. So you will typically find a willing audience.

The credibility and coverage provided by market analysts will help you establish a name and reputation for your product. By including analysts in your overall Market Validation process, and by using their input to directly affect your product design, you will give them a sense of ownership in your success. Believe me, they can be among your most valuable allies; a positive mention by a respected industry analyst can swamp your web site and inundate your sales organization. These are some of the happiest problems you can experience when launching a new product.

CHAPTER SEVEN
The *Ready* Checklist

Here's the summary list of the steps involved in a thorough *Ready* analysis. After you go through this checklist, you'll have a good idea of whether you're ready to proceed to the *Aim* stage.

I. DOMAIN KNOWLEDGE: WHERE DID YOU GET YOUR IDEA?

Objectively evaluate how much experience you actually have in your proposed market. Based on experience, I strongly recommend that you stick to what you know. Going outside these areas only makes your learning curve more daunting. You must know the subtleties of the market space, and prior experience is the best way to start gaining that knowledge.

Remember: The downside of knowing the space is that you might be tempted to take short-cuts. Be really careful here! Don't fall into the habit of getting comfortable with what you know from experience. You still have to go out and objectively gather the data you need.

2. THE MARKET: HOW BIG IS IT AND HOW FAST IS IT GROWING?

Figure out the overall market size and its growth rate for the geography you are targeting. Compare the market growth rate to the economic growth rate. If your category is growing faster than the overall economy, you're on the right track. If your category is growing *slower* than the overall economy, you are at your first decision point.

The approach you need to take when launching a new product is to follow the path of least resistance. Fast-growing, robust markets are like the incoming tide; they tend to raise all boats. The best way to look brilliant is to be in the right place at the right time, and this is a key indicator of that.

3. LIFECYCLES AND TRENDS: HOW ARE THESE AFFECTING YOUR MARKET?

Evaluate the lifecycle of the market you are targeting and the overall trends. If you are somewhere on the first half of the lifecycle distribution curve, you are in good shape. If you're on the declining back half of the lifecycle curve, you're at *another* tough decision point.

What trends are playing in your market? Are you riding waves of demand based on population trends? Do you have an innovative technology that will shake up your market? Know the macro trends that are playing in your market.

4. YOUR COMPETITORS: WHAT ARE THEY DOING?

Thoroughly evaluate your competition. This means direct competitors and substitutes for your product or service. In addition, evaluate the type of economic analysis your customers will do. Remember: When doing economic analysis, sometimes keeping your money produces the best return. You must be able to address this issue with objective data.

When doing economic analysis,

5. THE EXPERTS: WHAT DO THEY SAY?

To gain credibility for your opportunity, make the case with other people's data. Develop name-brand or other highly credible sources to make your business case for you. And don't forget, establish a relationship with a market analyst early on—it's a relationship that can pay big dividends down the line.

AIM—WHAT DO YOUR FUTURE CUSTOMERS THINK?

CHAPTER EIGHT
Aim

The Overview

You have now completed the first step in the Market Validation process—the *Ready* phase. Because the *Ready* phase is designed to go quickly, you probably analyzed more than a few potential markets. Now, you're locked onto a market opportunity and ready to invest more time and effort. The emphasis is that you've identified a market opportunity, not yet a product or service offering. *Aim* will give us the information needed to develop a market-oriented offering.

This step involves going beyond the surface-level information that is available to anyone analyzing this market, and develop a proprietary view of the opportunity. That's what will enable you to develop significant differentiation in your offering. In my experience, most companies who claim to be market oriented stop at the *Ready* step. It is critical to remember that everyone, from potential competitors to existing competitors, can readily access the information from the *Ready* step. To develop a truly unique and competitive offering, you must dig deeper, and in a way no one else can readily do. This is the key to product success.

Here's what you're about to find out: whether your target market is worth the investment in development and sales and marketing that's needed to make your product succeed. In the *Aim* process, you will invest significant time and effort getting to know all the subtleties of the market. And you will ensure that you develop your product around *what the market wants*.

The *Aim* phase is the heart and soul of Market Validation. This is where you go from a broad-brush concept to a fully fleshed-out version of what your ultimate product or service will be.

The *Ready* process was a quick-hit, back-of-the-envelope assessment of whether the opportunity is worth taking to the next step. It was a relatively straightforward process involving big-picture trends and some work with available data. If your market is a well-established one, chances are you gathered a fair amount of information during the *Ready* phase.

By contrast, the *Aim* process is far more in-depth. It assumes the opportunity you're pursuing, having come out of the *Ready* step, justifies a significant investment of more time and resources. In terms of a hard dollar metric, *Aim* will use the majority of the allocation of 5 percent of the development budget. Yes, it's from the development budget, not the sales and marketing budget. The idea here is you're investing 5 percent of your budget to make sure you spend the other 95 percent on the right things.

HOW *AIM* WORKS

The *Aim* process builds on the information from the *Ready* step and refines it down to specifics in your target market. This involves circling back to some of the data from the *Ready* process and further developing it.

More important, during the *Aim* phase you contact your target audience to confirm your current assumptions and to learn more about the market firsthand. Remember, during the *Ready* process you had access to the same information as everyone else. Now you're going to go deep—really deep—on the market opportunity. The only way to do this in a meaningful way is to do it yourself.

Two benefits: First, you will know the market intimately; and second, you will have insight no one else has access to.

The process is very powerful. Every time I've done it or taken a company through it, the results have brought the offering closer to what the market truly wants. The methods are not glamorous, but the results speak for themselves.

The big picture involves direct interviews with at least 100 customers in your target audience. These are the people who are your potential customers, and you will go through a series of interview steps with them. The initial interviewing will be around the market problem you are addressing, how much pain it causes them, how they address it today, and how interested they are in a solution. During these initial interviews, there will be no mention of your offering or any of the features or benefits you're contemplating. Your goal here is to get an overall assessment of the market, and understand the attributes of the companies or consumers who are experiencing the most pain.

On the second pass of interviews, you will close in on what you believe is the most attractive part of the market, based on the results from your first set of interviews. You will refine your target audience to make sure the level of pain and demand remains constant. You will test a variety of potential offerings and price points to gauge their relative demand.

On the third pass of interviews, you will focus on what you believe will be your final offering, feature set, and price point. You will be refining the details and confirming that the target audience remains constant as you probe deeper and deeper.

By simultaneously refining your product offering and your target market during these interview steps, you are actively testing your eventual sales and marketing strategy. You are refining both the offering and your target market, gaining more insight and further adjusting both to more accurately pinpoint what the market really wants.

Throughout, you use common market research techniques, but with a different slant. You are out to *gather information and understand the market pain* first, not to confirm that a specific product is acceptable. As you refine both the target audience and the offering details, you repeatedly check the market to make sure you are meeting its needs. Eventually, you will confirm that your specific offering is correct, but by the time you do this your product has been so shaped by the real-time feedback of the market you are really just doing a final confirmation. The key point is that, by successively gathering this information before the product is fully developed, you have the option to change it and confirm the changes before finalizing it. This is different from traditional market research, which is typically performed to confirm an offering versus shape an offering. Here, the approach is very different—and so are the outcomes.

THE RESULT OF *AIM*: A ROBUST OFFERING

I have used this technique dozens of times, within established companies and start-ups alike. As a result, the offering that emerges looks more like a generation-two or -three version in the eyes of the market, despite being the company's first release. In several instances, I have also used this technique to determine which of multiple product offerings made the most sense to pursue out of the gate.

In all cases, the first release of the products or services wound up significantly different than was first envisioned. In general, the products have been simpler and focused on narrower markets than the team originally planned to target. The results? Simplified development, focused sales and marketing, and faster time to market, all of which ensured that the company could rapidly iterate its product and pursue additional markets.

CHAPTER NINE

Research

Learning What You Really Need to Know

When the rubber is about to hit the road and you are seriously considering building your product, primary research is the only tool you should rely on.

As its name implies, primary market research is a close cousin to secondary market research. The difference is that you directly undertake primary research to understand key issues that are specific to your offering.

PRIMARY MARKET RESEARCH: YOUR #1 TOOL

With secondary research, you do not directly perform the interviews, and the information is limited to an overview of the opportunity. This information is widely available to everyone, so it provides you with no real proprietary insight to the opportunity. It is designed to be used only in the *Ready* phase.

Secondary research does not enable you to accomplish what primary research does: a competitive and proprietary offering, one that arises from a unique and differentiated approach to the market. With primary research, you can discern, explore, and validate *your own* opportunities, versus developing ordinary products that anyone can come up with after reviewing generally available secondary research.

The key attribute of primary market research is the desire for objective, unadulterated market feedback. This is intuitively obvious, but in the context of figuring out whether your product approach is viable, it can be one of the most exhilarating—and most feared—parts of developing a new product. Properly executed, the results are invaluable. From my experience with many, many market validation projects, I can tell you that the market never lies. You might not like what it says, or you might feel you can power your way through the issues, but in my experience it has never failed to deliver the truth.

With primary research, you work your way up to a point where you are actually testing market validity for your product *before you have built it*. In effect, you are test-selling your product in a number of different flavors to a group of customers before the product even exists.

Usually, after a statement like that, I get a bit of recoil. The thought of selling something frequently conjures up images of used-car salesmen with bad hair and loud polyester suits glad-handing customers into cars they don't want. The critical point here is this: It is far easier to get customers to spend time with you answering market research questions about something that matters in their business or personal life than it ever is to sell them something. You will face much less rejection when surveying the market than you ever will when selling a product. My advice for you is to enjoy the luxury of doing market surveys while you can; once your product is available and you are actually selling it, customers will never be as interested in talking to you as when you were just figuring out the market.

As we're about to see, there are countless ways to conduct these surveys. I will cover all of the techniques and explain and how to execute them as you move through the validation process.

The type of interview you use is an important factor. As I've discussed, we want to finish with at least 100 direct interviews. All of them need to be conducted live, either over the phone or face to face. Live interviews enable you to gather both quantitative information, which is critical to sizing and understanding markets, and more qualitative responses—what I like to call the "color commentary"—which, combined with quantitative data, is critical to getting the right kind of product out the door.

It is also important that you collect additional data through alternative sources, like online surveys. These ultimately don't count in your target of 100 direct interviews. I will outline when and how to use these other types of surveys in this section.

TYPES OF PRIMARY MARKET RESEARCH

You can conduct primary research using any number of methods, as long you collect the data directly from the market and ensure that the team performing the Market Validation work is analyzing and using the data. In the following sections, I'll walk you through what I've found to be the most effective techniques for gathering this kind of information.

FACE-TO-FACE INTERVIEWS

Face-to-face interviews are ideal and the gold standard for Market Validation. They allow direct interaction, enable you to read body language, and provide the perfect venue for probing along lines of thought that present themselves. Serendipity precedes great insights, and face-to-face interviews lend themselves well to serendipity. They are my preferred method because of the insight that they provide. You have the structure of a questionnaire to anchor the subject matter, combined with a free-flowing conversation that leads to great insights.

This type of interview is also the hardest to pull off. It requires a time commitment on the part of the interviewee, typically an hour, and that is significant in anyone's schedule. My experience has shown that, if you are solving a significant pain point, people are more willing to sit down and spend time with you. In fact, your ability to conduct face-to-face interviews is a good indicator of how big a problem the target audience has.

Face-to-face interviews are not only time consuming, but they can also be expensive. To get any type of geographic diversity, you will need to invest in travel to conduct some of the interviews. You can also expect a certain number of cancellations, further complicating the scheduling and expense. So the power of these interviews is somewhat offset by their low efficiency and high expense.

My preferred technique is to conduct at least 20 percent of the direct interviews face to face.

Whenever conducting any style of direct interviews, it's important to use a standard set of questions that all interviewees are taken through. All of the questions need to be answered completely to be counted as an interview where the data can be used; or, stated another way, you need to have a completed survey to be counted against your metric of at least 100 interviews.

In making sure complete interviews are conducted in a face-to-face environment, technique matters. You are really having a conversation with the interviewee, and not just filling out a questionnaire. Your goal is to develop a relationship with the person for programs that will be developed with a subset of interviewees as we progress through the Market Validation process. In order to develop a relationship and rapport with them, you need to conduct the interview as a conversation versus a process of walking them through a series of mechanical questions and answers.

In my experience, this involves two things. First of all, you should have conducted a number of phone-based surveys (techniques for phone-based surveys will be covered in the next section). After conducting a few of these you will be familiar with the questionnaire and the progression of the questions. In a face-to-face environment, I like to have a conversation with the interviewee that is relatively unstructured, but that includes points that are data to be collected. After I've accumulated two or three responses, I let them know I need to record some data, break eye contact for as briefly as I can to fill out the responses, then continue with the unstructured conversation. I find this approach leads to a more free-flowing conversation, which in turn gets the interviewee to expound more on the market pain I am addressing. When the interview is close to complete, I will review the responses I've gathered, possibly confirm a few responses to make sure I got them right, and ask any questions that I did not have a chance to cover.

The key value of the face-to-face interview is free-flowing dialog that is anchored by the structure of the questionnaire. I find these free-flowing, serendipitous conversations to be where real discoveries are made. These bursts of insight, in my experience, lead to real breakthroughs for your offering, and they are the reason I value face-to-face interviews so highly.

PHONE SURVEYS

In my experience, the best bang for the buck comes from telephone-based interviews. They can be accomplished in a productive manner; most people, particularly those with a problem you are potentially solving, are open to them; and the only incremental expense is that of the next phone call. Just as with face-to-face interviews, people's willingness to spend this time with you is a good indicator of the level of pain they associate with the problem.

Phone interviews have a number of important advantages. Given their interactive nature, phone interviews lend themselves well to the qualitative, color-commentary issues you want to discuss with potential customers, just as face-to-face interviews do. You can easily establish rapport, follow up on serendipitous comments, and take good notes during the conversation.

Phone interviews are efficient both for those conducting the surveys and for interviewees. Most businesses today are comfortable with phone-based interaction. In addition, interviewees will be more frank and forthcoming because of the lack of direct face-to-face contact, particularly as you are probing around a product or service area where they experience pain.

The other reason I really like phone surveys is that they will give you an early indicator of your sales process, something we will discuss more in the *Fire* section. Today, selling just about any product or service that is not a commodity or an established brand will, at some point, involve phone contact. Therefore, now is the time to refine your approaches and understand the types of phone interactions that work best in the markets you are targeting.

Another benefit is that phone interviews enable you to test the efficiency of your phone lists. A big factor in any successful product is knowing how many potential customers are in your target market, how to reach them, the sources for these names, and the quality of the lists. The phone technique lets you test all of this, including the response rates of lists. Information on list sourcing is covered in detail later in this *Aim* section.

One point that bears mentioning here is measuring the efficiency of lists sourced for various suppliers (again, covered in more detail shortly) for conducting this type of research. Yes, this process gives you an indicator of the productivity of your list source. The average response rates for any type of direct response effort, which would include conducting telephone-based interviews, is currently .8 percent (yes, that's eight-tenths of 1 percent). The math here suggests that getting one interview done requires going through 125 names. In other words, if you want one customer you need to make 125 phone calls. This is a number frequently underestimated by people launching new products, and it is important to know now whether you fall above or below that average response rate of .8 percent.

The follow-up to this point is, in my experience, you will get a higher response rate now, while you are only gathering information about your contemplated offering, versus actually trying to qualify customers or sell it. The explanation is simple: Individuals are much more likely to spend time with you when you are surveying the target market rather than selling the target market. A phone conversation introduced as collecting information will have a much higher response rate than a call trying to sell a product.

Similar to direct, face-to-face interviews, the most important benefit of phone interviews is the color commentary and serendipity that the phone enables. As discussed, when you conduct interviews it is important to use structured questionnaires with all interviewees. Over the phone, you can do this while also allowing the interviewee to expand on answers and provide valuable insight to subtleties—issues and concerns that can never be captured in a structured way. The phone enables this, like the face-to-face interview does, but on the phone you can record responses much more easily. Good interviewers can ask the right kind of open-ended questions that can get the target audience talking about their needs. As with face-to-face interviews, it's when your target audience is effusive and expansive that you can uncover strong ways to differentiate your offering in the market.

One downside to phone interviews is, like all forms of communications today, that many people simply feel overwhelmed by the medium. On the positive side, now is the time to figure out how dramatic this push-back is in your target audience, and figure out ways to respond to it.

The other potential downside to phone interviews is time. In my experience, most people get pretty restless after 15 or 20 minutes of questioning. You can manage this in two ways. The most obvious is to limit the number of questions. Although this sounds easy, once you see the power of the data you are collecting and experience how much work it is to successfully conduct one interview, you will want to ask many questions. The second way is to refine your target audience before conducting phone interviews using Internet-based surveys, which I discuss more fully in the next section. In an Internet survey, you can either ask people to self-select for more in–depth interviews, or find a target audience that experiences a higher level of pain and is therefore more willing to spend time helping you shape a solution.

You can use the same questionnaire for both face-to-face and phone interviews, so you can get double duty out of developing and testing the questions.

INTERNET SURVEYS

Electronic surveys are useful for collecting large amounts of quantitative information quickly and efficiently. They are a good way to start the primary research process and establish a quantitative base of information. If you can work your contact lists and gain a viral effect, it can lead to a large number of responses, giving you even better results.

Internet surveys establish the foundation for more targeted direct interviews to follow. With these surveys, you are really trying to segment your different target markets by their discernable characteristics to understand where market opportunities are highest and develop target audience demographics to go after with direct interviews. These surveys produce large volumes of data that are useful for this type of market segmentation; but, since they lack some of the color commentary that goes with direct interviews, you cannot rely on them as your sole source of primary data.

You can easily quantify demographic information for both consumers and businesses with Internet surveys. You can quickly gather large quantities of consumer information, such as age, education, income, location, usage patterns, preferred locations to buy, economic requirements of your offering and other factors. Business buyer information, such as company size, departmental attributes, and the buying process, can also be obtained. Combining these facts with indicators of demand gives us the required demographics to further refine our target audience using direct interview techniques.

The downside of electronic surveys is the lack of personal contact that gives you a qualitative feel for the respondent's situation. You can garner large amounts of quantitative data, but you don't have an opportunity to really dig into respondents' opinions. So, when using electronic surveys it needs to be reinforced that they provide data to segment your target audience, but not data on which to build the differentiation of your offering.

Overall, I like the large volume of information that can be gathered with these surveys, but I would not want to make any critical decisions without some kind of confirmation through direct interviews.

There are many easy-to-use web sites that enable you to set up, collect, and interpret data. You can use many sites' services for free if you send the survey to only a few people or ask only a few questions. This is a good way to experiment with these sites. Even if you are budget constrained, paying for the full versions of these products is usually inexpensive and very effective.

Given the quantitative nature of this data, I find these types of surveys to be useful and necessary extensions of the *Aim* process. I like to use them as frequently as possible to gather large volumes of responses. I do not, however, count them toward the 100-interview metric we've discussed. They simply are too quantitative; they do not provide the color commentary, interaction, or serendipity of a face-to-face or over-the-phone interview.

OTHER TECHNIQUES

There are many other ways to sample potential customers in your target audiences using techniques that are well known to market researchers and statisticians. I believe they have their use, but I find there is no real substitute for the two preferred direct methods—face-to-face and phone interviews.

Focus groups are a great example of another technique. They are fascinating to watch and I have experienced many of them. From a market research viewpoint, I think they have their use when you are trying to finalize and fine-tune a product. Asking focus groups to prioritize packaging options or advertising copy, or to finalize price points and color options, are useful functions at the final stages of a product offering. I find, however, that they have limited use in the product design phase.

The reason behind this is that focus groups have some major downsides in the early product development stages. The big-picture issue is that you are trying to size the opportunity of a market pain you can address, and to do this correctly you need access to a lot of data, meaning a lot of people in your target audience need to be interviewed at a detailed level. Focus groups go after representative samples, trying to get a small part of the market to speak for the broad market, something I find dangerous when trying to develop a product.

They also tend to suffer from group-think. Typically, one or two strongly opinionated people aggressively put forth their views, and the group tends to fall in line behind them. In relatively loosely structured meetings, with people who did not know each other before the event, communications and inter-action can be difficult, and sometimes people compromise their opinions in the interest of fitting in with the group and getting to closure on the issues.

Focus groups also tend to be fairly expensive. For diversity, they need to be conducted in multiple cities. Most companies do both coasts and the middle of the country in the United States, the idea being that these represent the three major U.S. geographies. In addition, focus groups usually require a specialized person to conduct them, and they are run in specialized facilities with one-way glass and lots of recording equipment. Typically, the attendees are also compensated, as the events can take several hours. All this adds up to a cost of about $10,000 a session, and, for three sessions, you can conduct a significant number of direct interviews using the Market Validation approach.

On a side note related to focus groups, one reason I don't like paying people for their opinions is that, in my experience, if people have a real need for a product or service, if that need is compelling, they are very generous with their time. They are more than willing to offer information that can shape a product that could address their pain. Although compensating people may get you to 100 direct interviews more quickly, I feel it's a false economy because it gets away from assessing objective market needs. As expressed earlier, your target audience's willingness to spend time discussing the problems you will be solving is an early indicator of the strength of demand for your offering. If interest is tepid enough that you have to pay people to talk to you, you'll have to do even more to get them to buy the product. That is not a good sign.

DIRECT INTERVIEWS:
A REAL-WORLD EXAMPLE

I have a great experience to relate that reinforces some of the points covered here. It shows how direct interviews can provide an excellent gauge of your target audience's pain; how your target audience's receptivity to being interviewed gives an excellent early indicator of eventual demand; and how being in touch with the market can make you aware of competitive moves before they are general knowledge.

The Market Validation effort was around an industrial waste treatment process that used a new form of filtration system that provided a significant cost reduction over the current standard. The new filtration company was in the early stages of conducting phone-based interviews to establish baseline market requirements. They found stronger-than-expected interest in more in-depth interviews. Obviously, they were pleased with the response, if not a little curious about what was driving it.

During one of those interviews, the interviewee agreed to do the interview as long as they could spend time speaking with the interviewer to understand what they knew about the market. In that conversation the interviewee dug deeper into the filtration company's status and was very interested in their new approach. The company being interviewed pressed for more details and a product sample to run tests. The filtration company disclosed that they were still validating the market and had not yet gone into production. The company being interviewed pressed for as many details as possible about the approach, its availability, and cost.

Clearly, the interviewing company had available none of the details the potential customer needed, and they let the potential customer know this. The potential customer requested that the company come out to their facility, review their approach, and make a recommendation based on their domain knowledge on how their new filtration system could be implemented. At this point the interviewing company had to let them know that was not possible, given the early, fledgling state of the company and its current focus on validating the market before proceeding.

To make a long story short, the potential customer eventually offered the company a consulting contract, including travel expenses, to come out and evaluate their system and explore how the new filtration system approach might be used. Although this was not part of the filtration company's focus at the time, and could have been viewed as a distraction, they felt it was worth the time investment, given that they would gain knowledge from the exercise along with a stronger customer relationship—not to mention they were also being compensated for their time.

In the end the trip was enormously successful. The filtration company learned firsthand about the potential customer's system and the operational details of how a new system would be put in place. The filtration company also learned, by being on site and establishing a relationship with the company, that the product they were replacing was being phased out. This was invaluable competitive intelligence that explained the high degree of interest by their potential customer base. It was also an impetus to get a simpler system out sooner to meet the market demand caused by the incumbent supplier. This potential customer became an advisor to the company as they further developed their system and was one of the company's first customers.

Needless to say, this type of response is invaluable. All of your market interactions will not be of this magnitude, but they will yield invaluable information on the real-time pulse of your market in a way no one else can reproduce.

CHAPTER TEN

Interviews

Getting to the Market Pain

The real art of Market Validation lies in the interview process. You are objectively accessing market demand for your potential product. The key is *objectivity*, and objectivity is not always part of market research. In this case you need to make it part of your process. Your goal is not to force your product into the market and make it work; your goal is to understand the market pain well enough to deliver a solution that the target audience wants and that has differentiation from your competitors.

THE FUNDAMENTALS

As anyone who has been involved with market research can tell you, it can be conducted to confirm whatever the surveyor wants to confirm. This is simply a fact of life in the market research world. You will not be doing this. On the contrary, you will be getting unadulterated, direct-from-the-market feedback. You are obtaining your own raw data—not the data that has been gathered by others—so that you can develop your own analysis and interpretation. From that, you can build a market-driven offering.

That last sentence makes a lot of intuitive sense, particularly sitting here reading about it in a book. But believe me, it can be really scary putting your well-developed, heavily invested concept out to be mercilessly evaluated in the market. Listen up: The capitalist system is brutal; it takes no prisoners and has no regard for how much energy you've invested in your business. To repeat what I've said many times, it is far better to find out what the market thinks *now*, when changes can be easily made, than after your product has been built.

I will cover the three main steps of interview development here. The three major categories are the start, mid-point, and finishing interviews. All build on data from the previous steps. They take you from a broad market assessment, to a gap analysis of the market opportunities where you can test your top three or four conceptual offerings, to a confirmation of your final, chosen concept.

How you construct your interviews depends on where you are in this continuum. Wherever that is, you want to collect objective, unbiased market data to drive and refine your product concept. In other words, you are after the answers you need, which are the answers your target audience has, versus the answers you want.

THE STARTING INTERVIEWS: BROADLY ASSESSING THE MARKET

In your first set of *Aim* interviews, you want to assess the market opportunity by measuring the pain the market experiences. Ultimately, customers buy a product or service to fix pain—to address something that is missing or time-consuming in their lives.

The easiest way to make sure you are assessing requirements and not trying to introduce your own solution is this: Never discuss or mention your company, its product, or any of its features when you are in this phase of interviewing. This is a simple rule, but one you will find frustratingly difficult. Let me give you an example.

Let's pretend we're Apple computer doing our first round of *Aim* primary research surveys as part of our Market Validation process. The *Ready* phase was already done, and we know the investment in this next step makes sense. We are just after a market assessment, and complicating matters, since no one yet knows what an iPod is, as it hasn't been introduced, we can't use it as an example, or introduce its concept in our surveys. How would you do this?

The line of questioning might start with a question along the lines of, "On a scale of 1 to 10, how important is listening to music in your everyday life?"

This is a great question to lead with because it gives us the individual's self-assessment of music's importance. As we gather more data, we'll look for trends that correspond to people who rated this high versus low. The idea is to capture the demographics of people who rated this high; this indicates, at a general level, the type of people we want to target in interviews going forward. On the flipside, it's also important to understand the profile of people who rated this question low. First, it is important that you understand their demographics and whether these demographics suggest a systematic reason for the low ratings. Second, you need to understand whether the low rating is caused by issues that the iPod could address. Doing this could allow us to significantly expand the market—which, of course, the iPod eventually did.

Following the line of questioning, the next question could be, "On an average day, how many hours of music do you listen to?" This is another self-assessment question but gives us even more insight. First of all, it is an objective measurement, and second, we can assess any similarity or consistency with how they rated the first question.

The following is a continuing series of questions that give us progressively more data on music usage. At this point in the survey process, we are trying to do an overall assessment to see where there might be opportunities for our potential offering. With this particular survey, we are simply trying to gain perspective on the importance of music to this person. Eventually, as we interview enough people and establish a quantitative base of information, we will begin to identify any correlation between music importance and satisfaction with current music delivery systems. We are trying to see if there is a gap, and hopefully a large gap that is painful, between what is available today and what people want.

Questions to be asked include:

- Where do you listen to music (home, car, office, while walking, . . .)?
- How many music playing devices do you own?
  - Approximately how much have you invested in music playing devices?
  - What is your favorite music playing device?
  - On a scale of 1 to 10, how would you rate your satisfaction with this device?
  - What are your three favorite attributes of this device?
  - What are your three least favorite attributes of this device?
- What formats do your devices use (radio, LPs, CDs, tapes, and so on)?
  - Approximately how much have you invested in these formats?
  - What is your favorite format?
  - On a scale of 1 to 10, how would you rate your satisfaction with this format?
  - What are your three favorite attributes of this format?
  - What are your three least favorite attributes of this format?

There's a lot going on in this line of questioning, so let's break it down.

First, you notice how we never mention anything about Apple or an iPod, or any form of music delivery or technology. In theory, even Apple wouldn't have known what it was building at this point, and although we would have gathered data in our primary research about the installed bases of other music systems, this line of questioning gives us a clearer understanding of where these competitors are actually installed. This is useful data, far beyond what straight numbers tell us. We do ask a lot of usage information in a very short time, again trying to get not only a picture of how people use music today, but also what systems we're potentially competing with.

You can also see from the line of questioning that this could lend itself very well to an electronic survey. We are looking for broad usage trends, and since music listeners could be anyone with an email address (meaning music is available to any consumer; if we were building bulldozers it would not be as easy to poll people electronically at this point), some of the data for this survey could easily be collected electronically.

When constructing this interview, it would also be important to collect demographic information on the interviewee. Being able to gauge trends based on demographics would be invaluable. Here's a short list of some of the data that could be collected:

- age
- income level
- education level
- gender
- geographic location

You can see from this example that we are assessing usage patterns and preferences to begin to understand potential market pain around music usage. We are also gathering some fundamental demographics to see if there are corresponding signs of usage patterns and preferences. As we covered in the first set of questions, it is important to be able to map back to target market characteristics the associated demographics. This also helps us understand the profiles of people who have no interest in music, which enables more probing around why they lack interest; later interviews could reveal whether a new type of product could address the causes of disinterest.

We are giving life to the data we collected in our primary analysis of this market. It's great to know how many CD players are out there, but now we know what the penetration of CDs is in high- versus low-usage listeners. We can see what the CD usage patterns are by age and income level. With the combination of some broad secondary data, we gain a clearer and clearer view of the music user segments and how users' views change across a variety of demographics.

Since this survey is quantitative in nature as it is gathering demographics and mapping those to usage patterns, you can easily use Internet surveys to query the majority of respondents. Given that this is a consumer product with widespread potential usage, a large amount of data is appropriate (again, if we were analyzing the bulldozer market, it's a lot smaller, a lot more targeted, and we might not do any electronic surveys as most people in this market don't have workday Internet access). If we were to aim for 250 total interviews, it would be smart to conduct at least 10 using direct techniques and appropriate to do the remainder electronically. Keep in mind, since we are on starting interviews, this volume of direct interviews is appropriate; there will be plenty of time for more involved direct interviews.

When constructing interviews, it is always smart to run a few test interviews before finalizing the survey. In this case, an electronic test of 10 to 15 people and a direct test with two or three would be good. Based on the results, we would probably clarify some of the questions and shorten the survey. This is what typically happens.

Given that your next round of surveys will build on the results of this one, these results will give you a lot of insight into what kind of data to collect during your next interview stage.

When you start obtaining consistent usage data about the target data, you are finished with the initial primary research phase. In general, you will do fewer interviews for business products than consumer products based on the smaller target audiences of most business products and the less emotional process involved with business buying decisions. Consumers tend to be less consistent in their requirements, which this phase of interviewing will probably confirm. You can address this by simply gathering more data.

Beyond this rule of thumb on consumer versus business interviews, my only other guidance is this: If you are not beginning to see some consistency in results, you are probably targeting too broad a market initially.

THE MID-POINT INTERVIEWS: ANALYZING THE GAP AND NARROWING YOUR CONCEPTS

As you gather more and more usage information about your potential market in the starting phase of primary research, you'll begin to notice clear trends. At the mid-point, you are looking for high market pain around the way people do something today. You also want to know how they articulate that pain. Based on this you will be able to narrow your offering to two or three options, which will be tested in the finishing interviews.

The broader your target audience, the more appropriate the use of electronic surveys for this part of the interview process. Direct interviews are more appropriate for narrower audiences. The guidance I provided in the previous section applies to both types of interview formats. Under either circumstance, your goal is at least 100 direct interviews. Electronic interviews do not count as direct interviews, and they are typically used in the beginning phase when you interview the large volumes of potential customers needed to understand consumer markets.

Based on the results of your beginning interviews, you are now looking for gaps that represent user pain and dissatisfaction. Later in this section I will cover this analysis in more detail, but let me take you through, at a high level, the patterns we are trying to recognize.

In the case of the iPod questions we put together in the last section, we are looking for pain, or a large level of dissatisfaction, with current music devices and music formats. For a minute, let's focus in on two key questions:

- On a scale of 1 to 10, how would you rate your satisfaction with this (your favorite) device?
- On a scale of 1 to 10, how would you rate your satisfaction with this (your favorite) format?

In and of themselves, pretty innocuous questions; but in terms of Market Validation, this is the beginning of the trail that will lead you to understand the market pain. If we looked at the answers to this question, we would come up with a normal distribution in which we could discern the average, mode, and standard deviations of the responses. But what we really want to figure out is everything we can on the people who rated the *lowest* satisfaction on either question.

At this point we're not as concerned with why they indicated low satisfaction, or how to fix it with a product or service; we just want to see if there is any consistency in these people's answers across all the other questions we asked. For example, do they rate themselves high or low in their interest in music? Do they share education, age, or income levels? Do they tend to all be unsatisfied with a particular device or brand of device? If they're dissatisfied with their device, does this correspond with dissatisfaction with their music format? Later in this section, I will provide guidance about perceiving these consistencies.

In the case of the iPod example, you'll be looking for what they dislike most about their current music solutions. You'll be looking for where the market pain is the strongest, where the largest gap in the market exists between an offering and a user's dissatisfaction with that offering. For instance, is it that user most dislikes music in the car, or home or office? You want to see where that pain is consistently high.

Once you've identified a consistently high pain, you want to try to focus in on two attributes. The first is any consistent demographics associated with a consistent pain. For instance, do you find that people aged 25 to 30 mostly dislike their music solutions in the car? In the first stage of interviewing, since you are casting a wide net, you might have to look hard through the data to find this kind of pain; once you've found the pain, you're trying to track it to consistent demographics. In this set of interviews, you will focus in on that demographic and that pain to see if there is consistency in target markets, along with an opportunity that you can exploit.

The key to this stage of validation is constantly drilling down on your results to uncover trends. Sometimes these are not obvious; later in this section I will provide techniques that will help you go deep and tease out trends.

Part of the challenge of this section is not only finding market pain, but finding the consistency in where it exists. You might have to complete the process multiple times to find your answers. In the iPod example, we would be finished with this part of the process once we found several pain points in the market with distinct market attributes associated with them. This gives us what we need for the next step in the primary research process, which involves proposing a product and testing market demand.

The key issue that begins to show itself at this phase is the need to keep analyzing your data for trends, and if needed collect more data to develop trends. Trying to express all the techniques and methods for doing this is just impossible in a book focused on the practical applications of these techniques. There are many specialized resources you can call on to help at this point, and there are many other outside resources to draw on that will be covered later in more detail in this *Aim* section. The key point is, if you need more depth in this area, call on these additional resources at this point of your Market Validation efforts.

THE FINISHING INTERVIEWS: FINALIZING AND TESTING CONCEPTS

As we enter the last phase of primary research, we've identified multiple pain points and understand the attributes and target demographics associated with the consumers or businesses that are in pain. Now we will turn our attention to understanding the pain in detail in each target audience and to testing the strength of different potential solutions to address these pain points.

Our goal is to identify multiple product options and multiple target markets and, through a battery of additional market surveys, determine which combination of target audience and proposed products has the highest market potential.

We will rely on data gathered during the *Ready* and *Aim* phases. From the *Ready* phase, we have the size of our overall market, along with the available subsegments. These could have been determined directly through secondary data or, for markets without secondary research available, assembled by us through the use of other data used to extrapolate the market size.

Combining our original submarket data with the results of our early and mid-point primary research, we've been able to identify high pain in three distinct markets and map that pain to subsegments we sized in the *Ready* phase. So by combining data from the *Ready* and *Aim* phases, we know our market size, market pain, and target market characteristics.

Now we need to test all the product and market opportunities and prioritize which combination of market pain and target audience presents our best possible opportunity. This is our goal in the final stage of primary market research.

Using the techniques I discussed earlier in this section, we'll assemble sets of questions to determine the level of pain, and hence get an indicator of demand, for each of these market segments. Based on this, we'll prioritize which markets we'll go after first, second, and third.

You can take several different approaches to this step, depending on what you are trying to accomplish.

The simplest form of testing at this point is when you have one distinct market pain and you are testing several potential product or service offerings. The efficiency is gained in that you now know your target audience based on results from your earlier efforts. Given this knowledge, you can easily obtain candidates to interview using techniques that will be covered in the next section.

You gain efficiency from being able to test multiple offerings against each of the target audience members you are interviewing. With one phone call or face-to-face interview, you will be able to test descriptions of several offerings and gauge their interest using a relative ranking system, such as the 1 through 10 levels we covered in previous examples of interview questions.

The next step in the efficiency game is testing one distinct offering against multiple potential markets. This is less efficient than the previous example in that it is easy to test potential offerings but harder to contact users in potential markets.

The final approach is testing multiple potential markets against multiple product offerings. If you find yourself in this situation, it might make sense to go back a few steps in the process and narrow down either the potential products or the potential markets to a more manageable subset. The number of permutations here will be difficult to follow once the results start rolling in, so it makes sense to go back a few steps and simplify.

It's important to reiterate what we are after here, and that is understanding market demand before we build the product. At this point you will be under a fair amount of pressure in any business environment as you are nearing the end of the interview stage of Market Validation. Keep in mind your goal is to get the product you are shipping right, not to hurry up and finish. The process of getting the product right shouldn't be regarded as linear, but something that needs to be data driven to meet the goals of what Market Validation is all about.

As you prepare to conduct your interviews for this phase, you are after demographics of businesses or consumers that have the highest market pain—the largest gap between what they want and what's available on the market today. Your articulation of these demographics earlier in the process will now pay off.

Another technique that can serve you well is to circle back to some of the earlier interviews you have done. Remember my recommendation of keeping in touch with people you have interviewed who experienced extremely high market pain or were very articulate. At this stage of interviews, it can behoove you to approach them and interview them again, given that you now are talking about the features and benefits of your offering.

A caveat here: Circling back to previous interviewees can be constructive and add to your sets of data at this point, but, before you ask, you can only count each interviewee once, so it will not help against that metric of at least 100 interviews!

It is also time to circle back to some of those quality influencers, pundits, market research analysts, and other contacts influential in the industry whom you have contacted through your Market Validation efforts to date. Get back in touch with them and let them know you are incorporating their input into your product offerings and are finalizing the interview portion of your Market Validation efforts. As you will see in the next part, *Fire*, you are about to call on their influence capabilities as you get ready to commercialize your offering.

Also, at this point, as you conduct some of these final interviews face to face, it is very advantageous to have tangible prototypes or real-world usage examples to share with people you are interviewing. It never ceases to amaze me how much either of these techniques focus people's comments and input as they really begin to picture how your offering could be used and how it would work for them.

A final reminder as you approach the end of your primary market research phase is you are really beginning the sales process for what your final offering will be. The diligence with which you pursue these interviews and nail down customer requirements will pay off shortly as you enter the final *Fire* stage.

CHAPTER ELEVEN

Who Are You After?

Finding Your Target Audience

The main goal for interviewing during the primary research phase is to gather data directly from the market and analyze the data with your own lens. This provides an unadulterated view of the market and gives you insight beyond the generally available secondary research and into how you can competitively differentiate your service in the market.

Your goal? To find market pain and develop a competitive offering to address that pain. You engage in direct interviews to understand and articulate the market pain and competitive offerings, and then refine those theories until they become a reality in the market.

TARGET AUDIENCE FUNDAMENTALS

As you become more and more refined about your service and its features, there is a secondary benefit to direct interviews: Your interviews resemble, more and more, the sales process. This gives you a jump-start in two important ways. First, your interview list in the later stages of primary research looks more and more like a sales prospect list. Second, you start to understand the sales process, how to position and present the product, and which list and lead sources produce the highest market response. This is critical to your launch, which is an integral part in the next phase of Market Validation—*Fire.*

As I will discuss in the *Fire* section, in which you launch the product, successful products experience an almost seamless transition from the *Aim* to the *Fire* phases. Hence, the primary research process needs to be viewed as not only confirmation and refinement of your offering, but the start of your sales process as well.

Before going into the details, let me also put down a caveat on these interviews and list sources. The goal here is to divine sustainable market demand; that means a target market needs to be developed and confirmed, and this is the confirmation process. Many companies have reputations, or large lists of contacts, or executive relations in a market that may be related to a new service offering. Additionally, many people have long-standing industry relationships. The mission here is *not* to rely on them.

You cannot interview people who know your product or company unless you do not tell them what company is doing the interviewing. Doing so will simply skew the results too much toward overly optimistic or supportive responses. To be viable, you ultimately need to get to a product for which you have objectively determined market demand, without relying on existing relationships.

My point here is this: You need to be able to develop a market based on the merits of how well your service offering addresses market pain, and this needs to be a definable pain experienced by a category of people who can be found independent of contacts or other known individuals with whom your influence is high. There is no problem selling to people you already have an existing relationship with, but relying on them is not a sustainable sales model.

SOURCING NAMES

So where do you get the names of people to interview? I can always gauge the street smarts of a new product team when I discuss this issue with them. The simple answer is, you'll find the names the same place your sales and marketing team will find them once your offering is in the market. In many ways, you need to interview like you're going to sell your product. Not only will you get the product right, you'll get the sales and marketing strategy down as you're developing the product. The teams that understand this succeed; the teams that feel they don't have to follow this approach, and figure someone else has to worry about sales and marketing, fail. You need to build your sales and marketing strategy as carefully as you build your product.

The initial sources of names come from the *Ready* part where you sized and analyzed not only your broad market, but the specific segments you are targeting within the broad market. Now you need to get the names in those segments, and, as you're figuring out if there's product demand and what features are important, you're also figuring out how efficient your name sources are in reaching them.

There are several ways to generate names. Some are classical marketing techniques, and others are emerging social media plays. The following sections outline various methods.

MAGAZINES AND LIST BROKERS

The classic, tried-and-true method is to purchase a list from a magazine source that targets your audience. This technique has been used for decades and relies on the same system that companies ultimately use for marketing outreach and direct mail.

The majority of business specialties have publications of one sort or another that target them. Every industry from construction to retail, transportation to services, chicken farming to aircraft manufacturing—all have specialized publications, and typically more than one. Cutting across industries, most specialized functions within organizations also have publications that target them, from human resources to accounting, sales to operations, building maintenance to fleet car operations.

As you enter your primary research phase, you should have enough familiarity with your target markets to know what these publications are, and have some idea of which publications are the most widely read by your audience. This is the kind of information that reflects the level of domain knowledge you have about your target audience; it indicates the level of effort you have invested in getting this far.

There are multiple avenues into these publications and a few techniques you can use to measure the accuracy and effectiveness of their lists for your purposes. First, keep in mind, we have not fully refined our target audience and we should not expect a straight-line process that neatly progresses from getting a list to finding our target audience. We will need several sources of names, and we want to include samplings from multiple lists in our interview process to get the level of refinement we need.

You can pursue lists directly from your target publications, or use list brokers to inform you of the types of available lists and publications. I prefer the latter approach, because list brokers frequently have a broader understanding of the industry and can also give you an initial screen on the quality of the list data. Keep in mind that, if these lists are for physical publications, the only thing you can assume to be accurate is the mailing address. And since we are not mailing surveys, other information that is important to us, such as name, title, company name, revenue size, email address, phone, and so on, will not always be as reliable. Frequently, a list broker can give you some insight on list quality on this front.

Another option to exercise is a list sample. If you are serious about spending a significant amount of dollars on a list source, you can usually obtain a random sampling of a few hundred names from that publication to run some test calls against.

Usually, these names are purchased five thousand to tens of thousands at a time, and the price will be in the hundreds to thousands for this many names. When you purchase a list, you want to find out what the total number of available names is in the list you're using. This is important on a couple of fronts. First of all, remember that productivity on making phone calls to this list will be low; eight-tenths of 1 percent would be considered good. So, if you want to get to 100 phone calls, with a response rate of eight-tenths of 1 percent, you will need at least 12,500 names. It is easy to chew through a lot of names quickly once you have an offering actually in the market, so make sure the list source you are drawing from has a large universe and you are using up only a small portion of the available names.

Most lists come with options to select certain cuts of the data. So, if you have a product targeting Research and Development managers and you want to be able to refine the selection to test a more specific target audience, you need to be able to define a number of characteristics within Research and Development managers to get further refinement. For a study I recently conducted, we did exactly this and were able to cut the population of Research and Development managers by commercial organizations, government organizations, and educational institutes. We were able to get names by specific states and regions within these categories. We were able to see what kinds of locations one organization might have around the United States, and we were also able to select by the size of the department's budget. This information enabled us to test our target audience with a significant amount of refinement.

TRADE GROUPS

Trade groups are another good source for names. These groups are typically focused on some type of affinity and tend to be organized along industry or job functions. Your ability to obtain lists of members and their contact information will vary, but typically these groups act as central clearinghouses for information, and the type of data you will need is frequently available from them.

Groups for professional organizations that require ongoing continuing education, such as doctors, lawyers, or certified public accountants, often have trade shows at their education events. These trade shows, which I discuss in more detail later in this section, can be attended by vendors; frequently, they allow vendors to provide material for ongoing education credit. You should consider this as a way to get directly in front of your target audience.

I once worked with a team that was targeting architects in the United States. At the time, a list of all the registered architects was available free of charge and was downloadable from the industry group's web site. Needless to say, this was of considerable value to the team. Of course, a caveat is that other industrious business people could have found it too, so I would not recommend using it as the sole source for your targeted names.

Frequently, you will have to become a member of a trade group, or pay some dues, to be able to obtain more data from them. Usually, these fees are modest, and something your company will eventually have to invest in, so you should seriously consider it at this point. Additionally, if the trade group has a publication you might also be able to purchase their lists using a list broker, as discussed in the previous section, without the need to join the organizations. These publications also frequently publish submitted articles, and you might want to consider doing this to gain credibility and give your company additional visibility in your target audiences.

TRADE SHOWS

As you probably have guessed from the previous section, trade shows tend to focus along industries and job functions as well. There are innumerable industry trade shows for the computer and automotive industries, retail and construction, delivery services and insurance, as well as for most job categories, from human resources to purchasing. Your job in gaining domain knowledge on your industry is to know all these sources of names for your potential markets.

Trade shows frequently will provide you with a list of attendees with your registration. Sometimes people register just to get the names and never actually attend the event. Other times trade shows will sell the contact information of attendees, so all of these options need to be investigated.

In addition to sourcing names in your potential market, these are valuable events to attend to get the buzz of what is going on in the industry. Depending on the size and cost of the event, you might want to consider a company booth where you can directly interview people in your target industries.

An option that costs less than presence on the trade show floor and can produce similar results is a hotel suite at the sponsoring hotel; you can pass out invitations on the floor, welcoming people to come to your suite during or after the event. Offering things like cocktails and hors d'oeuvres while interviewing people can make you a popular destination for folks who've been scouring the trade show floor all day.

Another way to stay in touch with your potential markets and gain credibility is to find speaking opportunities at trade shows. These events will usually take vendors on as keynote speakers. Don't expect compensation for it, but if your company has progressed to a point where it has an interesting take on the market, or an interesting approach to a business problem attendees might have, events like these can be a highly credible way to increase your visibility as you get closer and closer to your final offering.

BROADER SOURCES

Our coverage until this point has focused on fairly narrow target markets—typically, businesses where we can segment by industry, size, job function, geography, and other attributes. These segmentations enable us to narrowly cast our efforts based on specific, clearly defined target markets.

Now it's time to turn to less targeted efforts—for example, for products targeted at individual consumers (like Apple's iPod) or those targeted at generic businesses (a great example here would be office supplies).

My experience here has been the opposite of what we've discussed in this section so far. When you are after a targeted business segment you are usually in a bit of a scramble to come up with a sufficient number of list sources to get the broad data swath you need to narrow your industry focus. I find the opposite is true when you go after broader markets.

The key when doing primary research for broader markets is to do significantly more data collection early in the process, using some of the highly leveraged methods, like electronic surveys, that we have covered. This enables polling significant numbers (typically in the thousands) of a big audience efficiently to develop a broad base of demographics and understand their issues around the market pain, as we did in the previous example for the Apple iPod. Once these demographics are developed, you can target the profile and get more quality, in-depth views using some of the direct interview methods we have covered.

Great sources for this kind of data are all over the place. There are many commercial publishers that can provide you with white pages in database format. Many times, state governments will provide, for a modest fee, census, car registration, and voter registration data, though privacy laws are making these sources less available. There are also services that will do mass emailings to their lists of consumers based on many demographic picks, such as age, income, geography, and so on. I recommend all these sources for bulk names as you develop the target demographics for your market. Once you have refined them, you can go back to sources that allow you to select target demographics, and use those more targeted demographics to drive your direct interviews.

SOCIAL MEDIA

As I write this book, there is tremendous upheaval in the world of many of the list sources covered in the previous sections. As print in particular gets less and less popular and cedes more and more market share to electronic media, we are seeing dramatic increases in the use of electronic communications, along with the rise of social media platforms.

Clearly, this trend will continue. However, given the momentum of print media in some of the affinity groups we have discussed, I believe those nonelectronic list sources will be viable for quite a while. If they were to be outdated, your primary market research name sourcing would switch to the same name sources your sales and marketing efforts would switch to for established products.

As social media becomes more and more popular, you see many corporations moving over to it, and frankly struggling with how to be nonpromotional in this blatantly noncommercial medium. I think this struggle will go on for a while, and whatever solution ends up being effective will be nothing like what we have for social media today.

The great news is this: As a company that is not pushing a commercial agenda, meaning you have no product to sell yet, you can leverage electronic media extremely effectively, making social media a great platform for Market Validation efforts. Positioning yourself as someone who is trying to learn more about personal use of music, or gain more information on the bulldozer market, or better understand how controllers like to manage cash in their companies, is far more amenable to social media than is pushing a product. Enjoy it while you can, and aggressively experiment to understand what types of approaches in this medium will transfer well once you do have a commercial agenda to push.

COMMERCIAL DATABASES

Commercial databases offer a final source for your lists. Your company can subscribe to these databases and obtain valuable information. Many offer trial subscriptions from their web sites.

Data offered by companies like Hoover's and Dunn & Bradstreet is not specifically oriented to market research, but the data can be used for those purposes. Typically, for example, you can easily obtain the names and titles of executives in a company that is part of your potential target market. Often these executives list their outside affiliations, including trade groups, magazines, and organizations for which they serve on executive committees. Astute teams can scour these names for the most popular trade organizations in their target audience, which becomes a good source for names that are in tune with their market.

Even sources like Yahoo! Finance will frequently list a company's senior officers and their backgrounds. Many trade associations rely on executives to serve on their boards and steering committees, and these can be a good source of contact information.

You must pursue all of these sources. While conducting surveys, I frequently ask people what type of industry or affinity groups, trade-shows, and publications they are involved with. This helps refine my data sources. Similarly, as you gather your own data and refine the demographics of your target market, you can optimize your efforts by knowing the types of groups and publications people in your target market are involved with.

CHAPTER TWELVE

Turning Data into Results

How to Practically Apply All That You've Learned

CONDUCTING INTERVIEWS

As you conduct your interviews, you will collect data in a form dictated by the interview method. Phone and face-to-face interviews usually involve written or typed notes. Online surveys usually collect the data in a database format.

Expect to conduct many different types of interviews using many different formats throughout the entire Market Validation process. I always try to incorporate some similar baseline information across all of the interviews; this enables me to go back and test interviewee profiles as I move further and further along the validation process.

For example, I always collect background information of the person I am interviewing. For consumers, this includes demographics like age, education, geography, income, and so on. For businesses, it includes such information as industry, size of company, name and title of the interviewee, departmental affiliation, and so on. As your data sources grow larger and larger, this enables you to go back and compare results across target market characteristics if you consistently collect this information in your interviews.

Another technique I always use is to ask the interviewee if they are interested in being contacted again. This helps on several fronts. First, people who have a real problem that your service will address are usually interested in seeing that service brought to market, and they will be willing to contribute their experiences as members of your target audience. I've found that people's interest in spending time in follow-up surveys is directly proportional to how much pain they're experiencing: Second, there is always a certain percentage of interviewees who are particularly eloquent and concise in their description of the problem you are solving, their understanding of the competition, or their articulation of how you can address the market in ways no one else currently does. I always put asterisks next to these people's names, and, when I'm facing a tough issue, I just pick up the phone and ask for their advice. These types of people also make great Design Partners, which we will talk more about in the *Fire* section.

ANALYZING THE DATA

Once you've gathered all your survey data into a database, it's time to start the analysis process. Libraries have been filled with the subtleties of analyzing the results of market research, and I'm not going to go into elaborate detail here, but I will give an overview—just a few things you should be aware of as you analyze your data.

We will assume that you have entered all the data for a survey into a database. For statistical reasons that I won't go into here, you need to remove any interviews that are not complete. If some of your surveys were done in person, some on the phone, and some electronically, you should have used the same questionnaire and have complete results for each of the interviews you are analyzing.

Some of your results will be closed-ended questions, in which you asked for a discrete answer like a yes or a no, or a numerical rating on a fixed scale. Other fields will be open-ended questions in which you asked people for their free-flowing comments.

On the surface level, merely getting the data into a simple analysis tool like a spreadsheet can provide some quick and insightful results. Seeing which industries or size of companies have the highest pain rating, or what age and income of consumer is willing to pay the most for your proposed product, can be incredibly useful. Most business people are great at this level of analysis.

Given the investment you've made in gathering the data, though, I strongly recommend going deeper than a surface-oriented spreadsheet analysis. There are many ways to do this, including working with a market research firm or statistician to analyze the results. People who have worked with market research data can frequently tease all kinds of subtleties from what appear to be ordinary data.

For example, you can see if there are differences in surveys conducted by phone, in person, or electronically. Your overall data might show your product has a strong resonance with mid-sized manufacturing companies. By analyzing your results using advanced statistical methods, you can see whether in-person, phone, or electronic surveys pulled the most responses, and whether those greater responses corresponded to a higher likelihood to buy. Other tests can be performed to see if certain groups of interviewees had stronger responses, and why. All of these techniques allow you to tweak your ability to survey and get better results faster, which should have commensurate effects on your eventual sales.

INTERPRETING THE RESULTS

Interpreting the results is another area for which tomes have been written. My goal here is to give you an overview of the major highlights and encourage you to partner with some experienced market research people and statisticians to fully flesh out your data.

A main point, and one that is frequently lost on business people who are interpreting data, is the tendency to undervalue negative answers. Since Market Validation is not a linear process, any time an option can be eliminated, it should be viewed as a *positive* outcome. We may find that our hoped-for dual-income household demographic for our new consumer product does not want it; but in figuring this out we will likely have stumbled upon a demographic that is interested. And we learned this *before* building the product, which is always the goal of Market Validation.

Interpreting survey results is also critical to finding an over-all "average" level of demand in the above-mentioned product, for which we hypothesized our target market dual-income household demographic. Let's say the average demand for this demographic was a 5 on a scale of 1 to 10. A number like that might cause us to look elsewhere for a stronger level of demand. However, good interpretation of the results would cause us to dig deeper into the data, and we might find that, although the average was 5, it consisted of a clump of responses around 3 (lacking interest) and another clump around 7 (indicating high interest; this distribution with two peaks would be known as a bi-modal distribution).

The data could be incredibly revealing. We have a common demographic with two sets of very strong opinions—one strong on the like and one strong on the dislike. Using some of the data collection and analysis techniques we've covered, we can dig into the data and interpret the characteristics of this common demographic, teasing out exactly what causes the strong like and dislike.

USING THE DATA TO TARGET YOUR MARKET

Ultimately, your data on the area of the highest pain will lead you to a map of the market. In my first book, I characterized this as a "market heat map." When you create a heat map, you are able to draw a three-dimensional map of market demand that is color-coded to visually represent where demand, or market pain, is the highest. This gives you the demand side of what markets you should enter.

The end result you are after here is a visual representation of market demand by target audience. Properly analyzed, your data should be able to show you characteristics specific to your target audience across a number of different target audience characteristics. In the case of consumer products, this would mean axes on the graph with information like age, income, education, and/or geography that in turn represent market demand on a relative scale of low, medium, or high. For business-oriented products, demand on a low, medium, or high relative basis can be shown against company characteristics like size, the industry vertical the company is in, and/or the growth rate of the company. This data could be expressed in either two- or three-dimensional graphs. The main point of all of this is to provide a straightforward representation of your multifaceted data around demand.

Now that you know your market demand characteristics, you can take some of the other data from the *Ready* section to profile which markets you should enter and why. Entering a market does not always mean going into one where the demand is highest. Recall this from some of the subtleties we covered in the *Ready* section.

For example, using the growth rate numbers for the different market segments from our *Ready* analysis, we can determine which markets are growing the fastest. Using the competitive analysis from the *Ready* work, we can also see which markets have the strongest or weakest competitors. Using substitute analysis from *Ready*, we might also be able to discern which markets are ready to use our offering as a substitute for some other category of product.

USING THE DATA TO DESIGN YOUR PRODUCT

As you gather and analyze your data through many surveys, you progress from asking broad questions about the market to refining where in the market the most pain exists, to identifying which features would make you stand out in your market, to eventually testing out your final product description, feature sets, pricing, and options.

This entire process is driven by your primary research and the progression of your interviews from broad markets with generic demands, to subsegments of markets where the more specific requirements exist, to how to address those opportunities based on the knowledge you have gained in the market. The proper interviewing techniques, data gathering, and subsequent analysis are all critical to designing your product and further testing and refining it until it is built and ready for market entry.

CHAPTER THIRTEEN
Outside Help

Using Research Professionals

In doing the primary research involved in Market Validation, I have found it invaluable, when resources allow, to use outside firms in the process. I must emphasize here that the management team for the new offering needs to be deeply involved in the data gathering. This gets the team familiar with the data, gets them comfortable interacting with the potential target audience, and gives them working knowledge of the demand that is driving the product they are building. Market research and strategy consulting firms can augment these efforts while adding significant value to the process.

These firms frequently conduct these types of surveys, and their knowledge in constructing questionnaires, sourcing names, and conducting some of the interviews can be extremely valuable. In addition, they can provide significant insight and efficiency through their ability to objectively analyze the results of the surveys, interpret the data, and synthesize how all of this affects your product.

That said, if your budget is limited, you can frequently con-tract with market researchers on the interviewing front and statisticians on the results front for hourly or project work. Even on a limited budget, you should seriously consider this, given the efforts that need to be expended here to get the right answers.

In the end I want the company shipping the product inti-mately involved with the process for all the reasons just covered. For instance, as a metric around primary interviews, I want to see the team launching the product conduct at least half of the direct interviews.

CHAPTER FOURTEEN
Countdown

Preparing the Market for Your Product

We're close to establishing a complete picture of the *Aim* process. This phase involves a never-ending cavalcade of primary market research—research that refines the market pain you're addressing and determines the most suitable market for you. You then switch over to defining the product and features that address the market pain and your target audience. The *Aim* process develops the differentiation, features, and details of your product offering *before you've actually built the product*.

This last point cannot be emphasized too strongly. What I have described here is a bounded process that, when pointed at a market that has emerged from the *Ready* process, will help you determine whether there's a viable market to go out and attack. You have progressively defined that target market as you've gathered more and more data. This process does not guarantee you a market. What it does guarantee you is a full *understanding* of the market, with complete indicators on the market's viability. It's up to you to translate this understanding of the market into potential product or service offerings and test them as described in this *Aim* process.

In the real business world, there is a risk that you will have spent the effort on *Aim* and found yourself without a viable market. That is a very real possibility. Let's step back to first Market Validation principles: We are investing, up front, 5 percent of the development budget to figure out if there is a market for our product. If the answer is no, we may not like the answer. But we have accomplished our goal.

If the results are not positive, what are our options at this point? There are two. The first is to go back to the *Ready* process, run through that analysis again using the data we learned from our last pass through *Ready* and *Aim*, and see how differently we come out of *Ready* the second time through versus our first pass. If we find new viability from that exercise, it's time to go through the *Aim* process again with the updated approach.

The second is to understand that the key to success is fast failures. In this case we had a very fast failure where we didn't have to ship a product to get the answer we now know. In that case, it's time to move on from the experience and find the next market to validate.

CHAPTER FIFTEEN

The *Aim* Checklist

Here are the summary points for the *Aim* process. Once you have successfully completed these checklist items, you'll be ready to move onto the *Fire* step.

1. RESEARCH: LEARNING WHAT YOU REALLY NEED TO KNOW

The key part of Market Validation is objectively evaluating your market to understand market pain in detail. You do this by directly interacting with the market. The best approach is to conduct your own primary research by directly interviewing your target audience in person or over the phone. Both of these direct methods enable you to understand the subtleties of the market and to develop a differentiated approach to addressing market pain. The added benefit to this approach is that you are uncovering insight that is exclusive to your company and not available to other sources. Your metric here is at least 100 of these direct interviews during your Market Validation efforts.

There are other supporting methods that can be used to bolster these primary research efforts, depending on the type of markets you are pursuing. These indirect primary research methods should be viewed strictly as supporting methods that help you further refine your direct interviews.

2. INTERVIEWS: GETTING TO THE MARKET PAIN

The emphasis in conducting direct interviews is an objective evaluation of the market. Market research will produce the kind of results you want: a frank and honest assessment of the potential market for your offering. Based on this, all of your interviewing techniques need to be very objectively focused on fact-finding.

In conducting your direct primary research interviews, you transition through three successive steps, each building on the results of the previous efforts.

Starting interviews assess the overall market requirements by understanding usage patterns in your potential target audience. When going through this step, you assess market demands and do not test anything about your potential offering.

Midpoint interviews focus in on the proposed pain you are addressing and seek to understand how you can deliver an offering with differentiated characteristics to address this pain. As you finish these midpoint interviews, you understand the market pains you can address and what the associated target audiences look like.

In the finishing interviews, you are focusing more successively on your final offering and potential markets. You are testing multiple product or service offerings against several markets for prioritization of which combinations make for the most attractive opportunity. You are testing and finalizing feature sets, benefits, and pricing, and you are getting ready to start building your product.

3. WHO ARE YOU AFTER? FINDING YOUR TARGET AUDIENCE

The key to researching your markets is getting through to your target audience. You do this by employing the same techniques now that you will use when your product launches, and that means sourcing names that match your target market characteristics.

List sources exist in many different forms from many sources for both business and consumer buyers. These include subscription lists, trade show attendees, telephone book listings, commercially available databases, and list brokers. To effectively know your market, you need to know all the available sources, the quality of the lists, and the numbers of names available in the markets you are targeting.

These sources not only provide interview candidates during the *Aim* phase but also will provide lists of potential customers when your product is available. Because of this, you should track the productivity of these list sources while conducting *Aim* interviews so that you understand what types of lists and productivity you can expect when you eventually launch your product.

4. TURNING DATA INTO RESULTS: HOW TO PRACTICALLY APPLY ALL THAT YOU'VE LEARNED

The most artful step of Market Validation is turning the data you've collected into results. At this phase, you want to understand everything about your offering and your target audience. This is the place where that happens.

As you collect the data, it's important to gather consistent demographic information to be able to tie the different types of collected information back to the characteristics of a target audience. All of your data will typically be stored in a database format, enabling thorough analysis and comparison of differing data sets.

It's highly advisable to use statisticians and other professionals here, as extensive data analysis can frequently be performed on rudimentary results. Specialists can be of value.

5. OUTSIDE HELP: USING RESEARCH PROFESSIONALS

Outside research professionals can be a great deal of help beyond data analysis when it comes to performing the *Aim* step. Market research and strategy consulting firms have experience performing this kind of work and can be invaluable around questionnaire development, sourcing names, data analysis, and interpretation. Depending on your resources, they can be engaged at a project level or as point resources to help on specific tasks.

The important thing to remember when using these outside resources is not to have them do all the work. The team launching the offering needs to be invested in the data and should trust its sourcing. To accomplish this, never allow more than half of the interviewing to be outsourced beyond the team that will be responsible for launching the product.

6. COUNTDOWN: PREPARING THE MARKET FOR YOUR PRODUCT

As you wrap up the *Aim* process, you are really starting the sales and marketing process. As you finish, you know your target audience and the requirements of your offering. You know the pundits, industry analysts, and other influencers in your market. More and more, you have focused your features and functionality to match the market requirements. You know how to find your target audience and how to productively reach them.

All of the knowledge you have accumulated up until this point has not only shaped your offering but also provided you with real-time feedback to your sales and marketing efforts. Now that you have completed your checklist, these efforts are about to start. All your hard work and persistence is about to pay off.

STEP 3

FIRE—BLASTING INTO THE MARKET

CHAPTER SIXTEEN
Fire

The Overview

Finally, here we are—where it all comes together. You're about to apply everything you've learned so far. During the *Fire* process, the offering you've been designing morphs into a tangible product—one you can confidently launch into the market.

A simple, straightforward statement, right?

As you might have guessed, there's a tricky part. We're shifting gears in a major way. We're transitioning from gathering information to translating it into usable deliverables. And this stage, like *Ready* and *Aim*, has its risks.

Here's what can happen: The shift from information gathering to product development is not effective; all the material we've so painstakingly gathered and analyzed ends up on a shelf, and the team defaults to the stomp-on-the-gas-pedal mode to rush a product out the door. We've been single-minded in our focus on testing the market and identifying its attributes. Now, we delude ourselves into thinking that all that work was great and all, but now it's time to hunker down and build something—without regard for all the time and effort we've invested so far.

In this section, *Fire,* I will ease you out of the data gathering process and make sure your execution process leverages all the Market Validation work you've done. In my experience, management teams are usually really good at execution. The challenge is guiding that execution to the right set of business goals. And—you guessed it—getting the goals right means using *all* the results from *Ready* and *Aim.* If you follow the advice in this section, this is exactly what you'll do.

In many ways, the *Fire* process looks like any other product development and launch process. But in other ways, it pushes on some issues that go against how many companies actually act at this stage.

In this section, I strongly emphasize the inseparable coupling of development and launch. The simple truth of the market is that launch is more important than development; seldom do products fail because they don't work. If you follow through with all the Market Validation investment you've made up until this point, you will get the product right. Once that is right, the challenge is *letting the market know* you have a product. Given your strong execution of *Ready* and *Aim, Fire* is truly a critical leverage point. Do it right, and you will have a winner on your hands. Do it wrong, without a *Ready* and *Aim* follow-through, and you'll have a smoking hole in the ground—an *expensive* one, with your name on it!

As we've already discussed, and as many researchers have confirmed, your most important challenge at this point is to get enough resources to do the work right. And there are several other things that need to be done as well.

This section covers all of this in detail. First and foremost, it covers the management techniques that are needed to get a product out the door quickly. I'll talk about the critical need for a Market Requirements Document and Product Ship Schedule for communicating product functionality and availability. Finally, I'll show you how to accomplish an effective product launch and sustained sales and marketing efforts.

I reiterate that the entire Market Validation process is a structured, framework-based approach to a very nonstructured and nonlinear problem. The *Ready, Aim, Fire* methodology is like a funnel: We're taking lots of opportunities in at the wide end of the funnel and running an extrusion process to see what can make it out of the narrow end. To get from the wide end to the narrow end, one of two things has to happen: We either kill some of the ideas or concentrate the idea down by casting the opportunity more narrowly in the market. Remember this mantra: The key to success is past failures. Success doesn't come from muscling our way into a market just to prove we can make that market work. We want to muscle our way into the market of least resistance.

Ultimately, there are no structured guidelines to let you know when an idea should be pursued or dropped. As we have worked our way through each step of the Market Validation process, I have offered some rules of thumb on what kind of numbers you can expect and what constitutes an interesting opportunity. However, in the end, it is all relativistic to the market you are serving, the business model you are pursuing, your profit expectations, and, if needed, your sources of capital.

Before we dive into *Fire,* let's summarize your experience of the *Ready* and *Aim* stages.

In my experience, the *Ready* and *Aim* processes seldom finish on the exact same trajectories they started with. For example, in projects I've been involved in, the *Ready* step tends to finish with somewhere between 60 and 70 percent of the initial market hypothesis being accurate at a big-picture level. The initial hypothesis on the *overall* market is correct, but the *submarkets*, where we always want to point a new product, are usually different than originally hypothesized.

Circling back to the *Ready* process, this is why in that step it is so important to understand the overall market you are going after at the top level and to drill into and dissect that market to fully understand its submarkets.

To illustrate, let's take a look at the turbine business. Here, we have a large, multibillion dollar, worldwide industry. If you were to enter it using the Market Validation process, in the *Ready* step, you would break it down into all of its major submarkets: aircraft engines, power generation engines, pumping and compression machines, marine engines, and so on. You would probably also break it down by geography, given the need to install and service engines that typically drive widely dispersed, large, expensive equipment. You probably went into the *Ready* process with a list of what you felt were the top three markets, in priority order, based on some combination of application and geography. In my experience, almost everyone going in with one set of assumptions finds them changed. You're still in the turbine business, but your prioritized list of submarkets looks a lot different on the other side of *Ready.*

During *Aim,* you build on your results from *Ready.* Your interviews provide a great deal of detail and granularity. *Ready* is typically a quick-hit, high-level triage compared with the detailed and extensive direct interviewing of *Aim.* In *Ready,* you used data available to anyone with access to the information, with the main barrier to this information being the money required to purchase it. You discovered nothing that the world couldn't figure out, but you did get a more detailed and objective set of facts. As you moved into *Aim,* you built on this information by accumulating your own detailed, proprietary set of information.

The level of effort up until this point has been about 10 to 20 percent on *Ready* and 80 to 90 percent on *Aim.* The *Ready* process justified your further investment in *Aim.* Similarly, the results of the *Aim* process now justify the investment in *Fire.*

But keep this fact in mind: Your investment in Market Validation for *Ready* and *Aim* combined should have been *less than 5 percent of the overall planned production budget for the product.*

That's why I have to emphasize that before proceeding to *Fire,* you and your organization must make a serious business decision. At this point, you've risked no more than 5 percent of your overall investment in this new product. The process you have been through has produced volumes of fact-based data. Now, you have to ask yourself: Have you used the data in an objective manner?

I have been involved in many of these projects, many of which have paid off handsomely and some of which have resulted in complete failures. Almost invariably, one of two things resulted in the success or failure of each of the projects. First, the management team didn't know what the data actually meant until they had the benefit of hindsight; and remember, this applies to successes *and* failures. Second, the team ran into a serious roadblock or a big opportunity, and while this roadblock or opportunity was usually clear from the data, the team didn't understand its gravity until after they had a product out the door. Again, this can work for or against you. You have to be attuned and sensitive to *all* the results you get; you never know where or what the key piece of information is that can make a dramatic difference.

So, ultimately, you and your management team need to decide, based on the data available to you, whether you have adequately analyzed your results objectively. It helps if you've had outsiders involved in the process—particularly your primary research process. You can rely on these outsiders for independent, objective opinions and not use them to push through an idea that you need to analyze more carefully. Good research people will tell you what the data say. Because of this, they aren't always the most beloved group in business.

Are you with me? Okay then, here we go . . .

CHAPTER SEVENTEEN

Sales and Marketing

Budget for It

Wait. Stop. One more thing. Another big warning, but mercifully, this will be the last! This warning is integral to Market Validation. We need to stop and have a serious talk about budgets, new product development, and the always mysterious and usually ignored-until-too-late sales and marketing process.

I have worked with many companies that have a product or service that made it through the first two big steps of Market Validation, *Ready* and *Aim*. This is not to say that these were direct, point-A-to-point-B-via-a-straight-line trajectories, but the teams did the work, examined the results, tweaked a few things, and iterated through the steps more than once to arrive at a strong result. They probably iterated a few times on *Ready* and a few times on *Aim* until they really got it right and liked what they had. The data all looked promising; they found an opportunity for a differentiated offering in a market segment that had high pain, and they felt they could move expediently to take advantage of the opportunity.

Then, they stopped the Market Validation process. They felt they had spent enough time and effort on it. It was now time to put their foot on the gas, take off, and never look back. And here's what typically happened: They hit a brick wall—without any skid marks. Why?

Both the academic research and my personal experience point to the same set of issues: great, objective data combined with experienced management teams who could execute. The weakness always came back to this: They felt the hard part was done, and all they had to do was build a product. If you build it, they will come.

Unfortunately, in today's world, that is just not the case—not when new and better products are hitting the market every day, in every category. Up until now, we have focused on identifying a product that is objectively better in the market and focusing it on a targeted market. Now, we have to continue to invest. We have to design the product based on what we've learned. And we have to build, launch, and market the product we've worked so hard to design.

All too often, companies allocate enough money to build the product, leaving nothing for an effective launch into the market. Either they think sales and marketing efforts aren't important, or as the product gets more feature creep, in an attempt to assuage too many market requirements, they cannibalize the sales and marketing budget to fuel the development beast that's engulfing them.

How do you avoid this? My rule of thumb is simple: For the first year, budget the equivalent of your product production budget to your sales and marketing efforts. And don't build the product until you've done this.

Let me drive this point home. In math terms, 100 percent of the budget doesn't go to product development; 50 percent goes to product development and 50 percent to launch, sales, and marketing. If you doubt my rule of thumb, take a look at the competitive analysis you did in the *Ready* process. Any competitors that are publicly traded (or acquired by publicly traded companies, where you could dig in and find their early product launch financials) will prove this out. If private, reports from companies like Dunn & Bradstreet or Hoovers will show the same numbers. Don't whine; don't complain. If you can show me data that definitively say otherwise, I'm willing to listen. Beyond that, this is the formula to use.

Surprisingly, the cost of sales and marketing is seldom given serious consideration when teams conceptualize a new product. I find this is because sales and marketing costs tend to be somewhat "soft" and more difficult to quantify than the "hard" costs of building the product. The reality is that in today's hypercompetitive, hyperefficient global markets, *sales and marketing is more important than production*.

A rule of thumb to use is to allocate an equal amount of funding for the fully loaded cost of development and for the cost of sales and marketing. This assumes you will be spending aggressively to launch your product once it is available. It also leaves enough budget to assure a sustained sales and marketing effort over the first year.

This rule of thumb is designed to cover all types of business models and should be refined to reflect the specific type of product category you are entering. For example, in areas like technology and life sciences, you will need to budget *more* than your development costs for sales and marketing in the first year.

So, let's expand this point even further. You're a new company, or a new division in an existing company, and you've scraped together $1 million for your product. Your initial budget was to probably spend $800K on product development and $200K on launch, sales, and marketing. This is typically what I see for this type of company with this level of funding.

How should you think about the budget now? Your first-reaction budgeting rule of thumb was probably to think about raising more money, pushing the budget to $1.6 million, and leaving $800K for development and $800K for launch, sales, and marketing.

My counsel is a bit different. I would stick with the $1 million you already have and split that down the middle. Allocate $500K to product development and $500K to launch, sales, and marketing. My experience on this front as a guy who has run a venture fund is this: The team will only expand its spending, usually unproductively, when given more money. In this *Fire* section, I will outline how to get all you need from that $500K development and $500K launch, sales, and marketing budget.

By the way, for those of you who are already on this, good for you; for those of you who haven't done this yet, pay attention. On your $1.0 million budget, you have $500K for product development. Remember, earlier in this book I talked about taking 5 percent of your development budget for Market Validation. So, your development budget has a $25K dent in it at this point. The reasoning for it coming out of the development budget is that it helps you build a better product. So, your first step in the product development process is to spend 5 percent of its budget to make sure the other 95 percent is being spent correctly. Remember, the key to success is fast failures. I would rather have my name on a $25K hole in the ground than a $1 million hole in the ground. For the record, my name is on lots of both.

Are you with me?

CHAPTER EIGHTEEN
The Details

Write Product Specs and Schedules

When it comes to making sure Market Validation results get translated into effective products, there's only one approach I've seen consistently work. It involves putting both marketing people and development people on the Market Validation team, carefully documenting the features that will address customer needs, and following up with a well-documented production schedule.

Let me break each of these steps into its components.

Putting members of research and development and sales and marketing on the Market Validation team creates trust and confidence in the capabilities of both groups as they work together to develop the market requirements for the product. Their domain knowledge in their respective areas also ensures the realism needed to turn customer requirements into tangible product and service features. An added benefit is that their involvement in the Market Validation process, along with their collection of primary data through interviews, cements their confidence in the data. Their investment and trust in the process and in the collected data helps ensure that the data will be incorporated into the final product or service.

The effect on teams of conducting their own Market Validation work is always transformational. Once they see the power of gathering objective data and using the data to make decisions, it becomes second nature and a part of the team's culture. In fact, teams start *requiring* each other to back up their product issues with market data. This is the type of behavior you're after.

So, the first technique in this process is getting R&D people on a team with sales and marketing folks. Once they've collaboratively gone through the Market Validation process, in my experience, the team has taken the first and most important step to shipping and launching the right product.

What's more, you have a team in place with the combined expertise you need for two of the most important documents you'll ever produce: the product specification and the development schedule.

One important takeaway warrants repeating before you proceed. The key to translating all the Market Validation work that has been done is to have a qualified team doing the work, along with clear articulation of what that work translates into in terms of product features and a development schedule.

PRODUCT SPECIFICATIONS

It is absolutely critical that you create clear and detailed documentation of the product and its associated features—features that the Market Validation team has uncovered. This document goes by various names, depending on the industry you are operating in, but it usually is entitled the "Marketing Requirements Document" or "Product Requirements Document" and is frequently abbreviated as "MRD" or "PRD." Clearly, what you choose to call it is not the issue; the issue is that it exists.

Assuming a Market Validation team comprising both research and development and sales and marketing backgrounds, sales and marketing usually takes the lead on this document. The highest-functioning teams I have worked with take this approach, with the added step of having the development part of the team sign off on the requirements document. This means, by reference, that the development side of the house can understand how the product specification was arrived at, based on their familiarity with the data used to assemble it. It means they agree with the interpretation of the data and the ensuing translation into market requirements. And importantly, it means there is enough articulation in the document for the research and development team to be able to translate it into the required features that will need to be built.

Don't expect this sign-off process to happen on the first pass. The important thing is that the R&D and S&M team members challenge each other for clarity and transparency on how Market Validation results have driven the product specification and that both parties agree to what is said in the finalized document. When I lead teams through this process, I have everyone sign and date the final document in a final sign-off meeting.

The sign-off process ensures that both parties commit to the feature set as specified. The subtleties within this commitment include some of the points that will be discussed in the following sections. The specification sets forth what the minimally acceptable features are; that means the product is not ready until those minimal features are finished. The specification also supports getting a product to market as quickly as the minimum feature sets can be built. Finally, it reflects the level of quality needed to meet market requirements. As will be covered later in this section, quality levels need to be considered as integral to product shipment and need to be specified in this document.

An exercise that I like to do around product specifications is for the team to engage in a prioritized ranking of all the features, even if all the features are in the must-have category. When you do this before the development process starts and the going gets tough, you have an objective touch-point to reach back to. A prioritization, even of features that must be in the product, provides guidance as to how much effort should be expended on a relative basis. In a nutshell, all the features are required, but if they are all of equal importance, then none of them are *really* important. So, this prioritization effort is very constructive at this point in the process.

Anyone involved with the product specification and development process understands how straightforward everything in the last paragraph sounds but how hard it is to implement. In having the Market Validation team document the requirements, your goal is that they will hold each other accountable for delivering the product as specified. By carefully documenting and prioritizing what that is before the development process starts, we are taking advantage of the fact that the team is close to the customer requirements and the data driving them at this point in the development process. Once development starts and the inevitable schedule pressure seeps into the process, it is harder to be objective in prioritizing features.

PRODUCT SCHEDULES

As you engage the process of getting the right product out in the *Fire* step, your next must-do is a product development schedule. Similar to the product specification, the exact term for this document differs, depending on your industry. The typical generic term will be something like the "Product Delivery Schedule." The semantics are not the issue. What's at issue is that the document exists.

Just as with the Product Requirements Document, it is critical that the development schedule be created by a high-functioning Market Validation team consisting of development and marketing resources that have been through the validation process together. This time, development takes the lead, mapping out a production schedule based on the features documented in the product specification.

The highest-functioning teams I have worked with on this process also cost out the development, and subsequent quality assurance time, for each of the product features outlined in the product schedule. This results in a clear-cut list of features, with specific development and question-and-answer times for each. There will always be subtleties around costing out what a feature really takes, but development needs to be able to attach time costs to each feature in the same way that marketing prioritized the importance of each feature. We are not striving to micromanage a development schedule, but we do need to know what each set of features costs, in terms of development time, in order to meet our goal of fast time to market (which will be covered in detail later in this section).

One key clarification: It is highly desirable to have a product development schedule impact the product specification document. With all dynamic processes, a stake has to be put in the ground to provide a stable set of variables to figure out a dynamic problem. In this case, at this point in the Market Validation phase, our most stable set of data comes from the results of our Market Validation efforts. The Market Validation team locked down a minimal set of features that a selected market wanted so that development could come up with a production schedule.

If the development schedule reflects a timeline that undermines the fast-time-to-market goal, the team must go back and reevaluate product features and target markets. The goal of getting a product out quickly is paramount to product success, and you must view developing the product specifications and development schedule as a dynamic, give-and-take process. It's a process that highlights the true interdependence of the product specification on the development schedule and the development schedule on the product specification.

The scenario goes something like this. A set of features was locked down, with the goal of hitting a clearly defined submarket. The submarket was well understood, and based on the results of Market Validation, it was clear that the market demand was going to be strong for the next nine months, with a key competitor expected to enter within four months. This meant the team had to produce a product to enter this market within three months, and this was documented in the feature requirements.

The development side of the team went to work and found that shipping the minimally acceptable feature set (more on what this term means is found in following sections) would take five months.

This represents a conundrum. To hit this market, meet customer requirements, and beat a competitor's offering, you need a product in three months, and since the delivery schedule has nothing in it but the minimally acceptable feature set, the delivery schedule can't be shortened to less than five months. What should be done?

First, remain calm! Knowing this now is excellent news. What's more, it's a fine example of Market Validation in action. Most teams wouldn't have figured this out until they had failed in the market; in addition, they would probably not *ever* uncover the true cause of the failure.

It's time for the Market Validation team to put their heads together and figure out their options, which are many at this point. Again, given the Market Validation process, none of the serious money has yet been spent on development and launch. And until this ship date situation is resolved, it won't be.

Here are a few illustrative examples of what might be done.

First, the team could choose to remain in the same market and hit a later ship date. They would need to reevaluate their Market Validation data, understand what has changed about the situation that enables them to accept a later ship date, and estimate the impact of the later ship date to the business plan.

Second, the team could remain in the same market and hit the more aggressive date with a reduced feature set. Compensation for the reduced feature set could be addressed through partnering deals, reduced pricing, or reduced market expectations about the product. Again, the team needs to go to work, assess all the options, and agree on whether this makes sense.

The third option is to go back, reevaluate the data, and target a different, smaller submarket. All of the data collected in the *Ready* phase can be applied here, and much of the data in the *Aim* phase can also be used to evaluate submarket options. The only data that might need to be collected again would be the data collected in the primary research part of the *Aim* process, where the team honed in more and more on the submarket that was initially targeted. This time, they would cycle back to the later stages of primary research and identify features that could be removed based on the new, even more focused submarket. They could then move forward with the smaller submarket as the target.

Again, the key issue is this: Thanks to the broad data collection that occurred throughout the Market Validation process, the team can use these data to identify an attractive alternative in the face of new information.

This process reinforces my assertion that we are applying a very structured process to a very *unstructured* set of circumstances. If the team is locked into a preconceived notion of what the product is and when it will be available, that defeats the fundamental tenets of Market Validation.

THE PRODUCT MANAGER

As you turn your product from idea to reality and begin building the organization to support all of this, it's imperative to keep one point in mind.

The job the Market Validation team performs will have a formal organizational function once the product is available in the market. Although different organizations and different industries have differing names for this function, what the team has done until this point is generically referred to as "product management." This team assembles and communicates all market-based data, and they're transforming the data into product features and ship schedules. The skill set is specialized and usually fairly unique. It requires the customer sensitivity associated with sales and marketing and the technical depth associated with research and development.

At some point, you will hire or appoint a person to take over this responsibility on an ongoing basis. Up until now, product management has described an intense and focused version of Market Validation. As the job function of Market Validation takes on a permanent organizational role, it will sit within the product manager's purview. That is to say, Market Validation should still be performed by a cross-section of the entire organization supporting the product and be driven by product management.

In my experience, the companies with the best products not only follow the Market Validation process as they envision and design a product, but after they ship that product, they also keep this same process alive in the product management job function.

CHAPTER NINETEEN

Fast to Market

Get a Market-Oriented Product Out Quickly

In this chapter, I'm going to expound on getting a product out the door quickly.

Some of you get what I mean, and some of you are taking a step back when you hear about speed and product releases. It's important to set the context here by covering the philosophical approach.

The best form of Market Validation is getting someone—an industrial or consumer purchaser—to open up their wallet and part with their money. The entire Market Validation process is a process of improving the likelihood that this will happen. A customer parting with their money moves the whole process from a test to something real: a product or service that's available and that has been accepted. The customer has voted with their money.

As you take this critical step from experiment to practice, the best way to stay focused on the market is to simply move fast. The capitalist world is brutally competitive, and capital flows to where it can make the best return, so don't take comfort in thinking you've uncovered a gem no one else knows about. You've got to move with lightning speed to get your product in the market as quickly as possible. As Andy Grove, the former CEO of Intel, says, "Only the paranoid survive." It's time to be paranoid.

In this section, I'll tell you how to do this. We'll look at a number of techniques companies use to get products out quickly. All of them reflect a philosophy I've oft quoted up until now: The secret to success is fast failures. At this point, our data suggests we have a product that works in the market, and now we're going to prove it by getting the offering out so that customers can vote with their money—fast.

You can take comfort that you're moving fast at this point based on all the Market Validation efforts you've put in to date. Most companies go straight to the *Fire* phase without much thought and stomp their foot on the gas pedal, expecting success. Following this metaphor, it's time to accelerate fast based on what we've learned but not stomp on the gas pedal indiscriminately.

MINIMALLY ACCEPTABLE FEATURE SETS

To move fast, it's imperative that you develop minimally acceptable feature sets for your target audience. In your Market Validation work to date, you've narrowed your target market to focus your efforts on a discrete set of features to address a discrete market. For your offering, this gives you a huge advantage: Because you've focused in on a narrow market, your goal is to satisfy a submarket before moving to the next submarket.

This approach is critical when launching a new product. Again, most companies will focus on a large market with multiple submarkets by developing a set of features that represents the average user in an overly broad market. The Market Validation approach requires a targeted submarket with a discrete target audience and a very specific set of features. This enables a shorter development cycle based on discrete—and therefore reduced—features. Your tightly targeted audience enables you to sell and market to this audience very cost effectively and to generate revenue quickly, providing the ultimate form of Market Validation.

As we're translating Market Validation results into product features, a very useful technique is to categorize each feature into one of two categories: "must have" and "nice to have." This technique reflects a focused market approach and further enables a quick development cycle. Prioritizing features in this way ensures that we can easily identify the minimally acceptable features for the first product. It is based on our Market Validation results to date from the *Ready* and *Aim* steps.

Realistically, I do recommend including *some* additional "nice to haves" along with the required "must haves" in your final product specification. I do this for two reasons. First, with a fixed ship date that is not too far in the future, the more product features there are; in addition, there is more room for feature maneuvering as we close in on the ship date.. Second, as anyone who has been involved with shipping new products or services knows well, nothing goes as planned. The more seasoned the team is, the more reliable the build schedule and ship date will be. The more accountable the corporate culture is to commitments, the more reliable the ship date will be. That said, it's always good to include some features that are *not* critical to market acceptance, if only to ensure there's some slack available for the team to make trade-offs between features and ship dates. This can best be expressed by asking yourself the following: Do you want it right, or do you want it Friday? Early on, we want it both right *and* Friday but with enough slack that we can always get it by Friday. Having a few features in a schedule that are not critical provides this slack.

For those of you who are still skeptical, let me point to a company that rigorously follows this philosophy when launching new products. By reputation, no one wants to use the first or second versions of its products. For its products that are successful enough to see a third release, that third release usually has greatly expanded market potential, building on what the company learns in the first two releases. This company has more cash on hand than most countries and has more development resources than any of its competitors. If it wanted to throw thousands of man-years at projects, it easily could but never does. It still ships a minimally acceptable number of features in its first releases; its second releases are a little better, and the third (again, if the product makes it this far) are usually accepted by the market.

The company? Microsoft.

Regardless of how you might feel about Microsoft, you cannot argue with its success. I strongly encourage you to take this page from its product strategy playbook.

FAST PRODUCT ITERATIONS

With minimally acceptable product features, our goal is not to tie up valuable time trying to build complicated products once we've finished the *Aim* stage of Market Validation. Our tightly focused features and target market will enable us to overwhelm the market with our product; part of that involves strong execution, and part of that involves picking the easiest market to overwhelm.

The key issue around fast product iterations is to remember that the ultimate form of Market Validation is getting someone to open their wallet and part with their money. The best way to do this is to get a product out on the market, with a minimally acceptable set of features—quickly.

The role of speed in today's markets is critical. Global markets are hypercompetitive, and the ready flow of capital to high-potential returns suggests that high market pain opportunities won't be there long. You have to move fast once you've uncovered an interesting opportunity.

This need to move quickly is compounded by the Market Validation process itself. As you transition from *Aim* to *Fire,* you have effectively frozen your feature set at what the market wanted the day you transitioned to *Fire*. In all likelihood, your market is dynamic and fast moving, so every day you spend developing your product is a day your market is evolving away from what your product is. You have to move fast and strike before the market shifts significantly.

As we've seen, minimally acceptable feature sets are one way to do this. The other is to take those minimally acceptable features, pare them down to something barely acceptable, and get a product out. As I discussed in the section on product life cycles, we expect lower volumes from narrower market segments when launching. People are anxious for a product and are desperate to address their market pain. Test and retest to figure out the skinniest set of features that are still viewed as viable in the market, and get them out the door as fast as you can.

Once the product is in the market, move aggressively to figure out what's needed to further penetrate the market, and quickly bring the updated version to market. By developing and shipping a series of minimally featured products at a rapid pace, you will be receiving regular, steady feedback on the offering's effectiveness. This approach is far more efficient than taking on a longer development cycle while your market is shifting, only to find market requirements have shifted significantly during the time spent in development.

An excellent example of this philosophy has been the multiple product iterations of Apple's iPhone. The original version was timed to have strong availability in anticipation of the holiday buying season. An often rumored and partially confirmed feature of the original iPhone was going to be a built-in global positioning system (GPS). This feature was dropped from the original version in an effort to make an earlier ship date. As of the writing of this book, the iPhone still does not have GPS enablement (though it does have a form of cell tower triangulation locating). The point here is that the market wants GPS enablement and will most likely get it eventually in the iPhone, but based on current demand for the product, the lack of GPS enablement is not hurting sales.

QUALITY DOESN'T ALWAYS MATTER

I know some of you have a quizzical look on your face when you hear quality doesn't always matter. I say it not as an excuse for shipping poor products but as a philosophical view of the product development process. Clearly, if you look at aircraft, heart valves, and car brakes, poor quality just won't cut it. But when used in the context of getting products in the market quickly, the definition of quality needs to be set in the context of how customers will use the offering.

What I'm talking about here is the typical product development process. Most companies start building a product and either test it during the development cycle or switch over to the quality assurance cycle and do their best to test and break it after it's built. As you add more and more features, this process has a compounding effect on the time required to test everything. In other words, the time it takes to test the product increases exponentially with the number of features.

As anyone involved with building a product and getting it out the door knows, each feature needs to be tested to the breaking point. Increase the number of features and you increase the amount of testing time proportionally. Then, the compounding effect of feature-to-feature testing comes into play and increases the testing time exponentially. One small change to feature A breaks features B and C. Fix B, and features D and E have problems. All of a sudden, the 60 days of quality assurance time allocated to test the product before the final ship date is nowhere near enough. What do you do?

Here's what: Use our fast product release and minimally acceptable feature set approaches. Indeed, follow these approaches religiously. Cut the features to the bare minimum, and you will have exponentially reduced your quality assurance time. Understand how customers will use the product from your Market Validation work, and you will know what features and combinations of features will most likely be used. Focus your quality efforts on those high-usage features and high-usage feature combinations, and move as expeditiously as possible into the market.

KILLING FEATURES EARLY IN THE DEVELOPMENT PROCESS

One of the key advantages of written product specifications and a production schedule is the back and forth in which the sales and marketing and research and development sides of the team can engage. An important byproduct, and one that directly affects the shipping schedule, is the ability of this team to kill product features as early in the development process as possible.

Again, let's look at the philosophical approach we're trying to take here. The overriding goal for Market Validation is to get the *minimally acceptable feature set on the market as quickly as possible.* Assuming we enter the development process with a very skinny set of features, based on the results of our *Aim* process, we're well on our way.

Once we've committed to the product specification and the delivery schedule, our only remaining leverage is to watch closely and to aggressively look for significant changes from what we were expecting. Experience has shown that these will come in two forms: changes in market conditions and changes to production schedules based on development progress.

Market conditions change constantly, and the process we're using is not prescient; it simply uses objective market data to understand market requirements, which in turn drive product features. As time passes during development, inevitably market conditions will shift, and the product we're building might have to react to them to remain competitive. My main point is this: Whenever you see the opportunity to reduce your feature set and pull in your ship date, do so.

The second reality of shipping new products is the real-time update of the production schedule based on production and quality assurance results. Seasoned teams of engineers and product personnel are the best at estimating production time frames, but the reality is that ship schedules seldom get shorter. In fact, they almost inevitably get longer.

Combine these two real-world happenings, and sometimes you'll feel the universe is conspiring to keep you out of the market. Philosophically, you need to look at both as totally expected, and you need to focus on removing, not adding, features. Your teams need to go back and reevaluate *Aim* results, scrub the development schedule again, and figure out what can be thrown overboard to make the desired ship schedule. Remember, features jettisoned early in the development process pay significant dividends in time as you near the end of the development cycle.

Just as increasing the number of features leads to an exponential increase in the ship schedule, removing features early exponentially *reduces* the ship schedule. You can expect "feature creep" and "schedule creep" along the way, and you always need to react aggressively when you see this happening. The simple fact is that removing features earlier cuts development and quality assurance time. Your savings are only compounded when you consider the reduced time of managing the often unpredictable interactions among features.

Speak to anyone involved with the development of a product or service, and inevitably you see a similar pattern as development comes to a conclusion. Lots of features and functionality are simply removed near the end of the project to meet the ship date. The result is a false economy of making a ship date without all the original features. Features removed at the end of the process mean that all the development and quality assurance efforts that went into the removed feature are wasted.

With a Market Validation approach, we not only ship a minimal set of features, but we have also removed the features before development started versus the far less efficient approach of removing them in the waning days of development.

CHAPTER TWENTY

Early Customers

Recruit Design Partners and Advisory Boards

Now that the product has been specified and is under development, it is critical to keep a close eye on the market, for two reasons. First, market conditions change constantly. Second, you need people in your target market that you can draw on for quick answers as you make product decisions during development. You must be able to gauge how market requirements evolve at every step of the development cycle.

There are a number of techniques you can use here. However, I believe the best way to keep your market focus during development with the least amount of resources and the most efficient use of time is to run what I call a "Design Partners Program."

The overall purpose of a Design Partners Program is to maintain active contact with a select subgroup of the people you have been in contact with during the *Ready* and *Aim* stages. These people are familiar with your product. Many of them have a particularly acute need for your proposed service or are particularly articulate in describing the business issue and the types of features and functionality required to address the market opportunity. I like to recruit these people into a Design Partners Program. I also like to recruit any key influencers I have worked with up until this point, including analysts, the press, and pundits from the industry or category I'm entering.

This group of people will become your inner circle of advisors as you move closer and closer to the ship date and product launch. On the development front, many times you will have to make fast product decisions about features that could be removed. (Notice how I'm avoiding adding features at this point—just don't go there!) To do so effectively and in a timely manner, you need a trusted group of confidants who are up to speed on what you're doing, understand the business opportunity, have good business sensibilities, and can articulate their ideas well. These people will be your lifeline as you traverse the product development tunnel.

As covered in *Ready*, as you interview analysts, members of the press, and pundits that support your position, keep in touch with them about the status of your new offering. Show them how you have used their feedback in your offering. Develop a plan to keep them updated, and when appropriate, recruit them to your Design Partners Program.

The same strategy holds true for customers in your target audience. As I described in the primary research part of *Aim,* keep track of potential customers who are particularly articulate and have acute market pain around the problem you are solving. These people are excellent Design Partner candidates.

HELP TO DESIGN THE PRODUCT

I like to start recruiting Design Partners around the time I'm translating the results of the *Aim* process into the features of my new service. The translation of primary research data into features and functionality can be critical. Many times, your domain knowledge can help—as long as you make sure this experience is not tainting your view of how a feature should be implemented. A way to assure this is through the use of Design Partners.

This is also an opportunity to get beyond just your target audience for the product and into the ecosystem that supports the product or services in your market category. You can go after industry analysts, the press, and pundits that have a strong working knowledge of your market. Frequently, these people can suggest different approaches to address the same set of features. They also tend to be very familiar with competitive offerings and may be able to provide you with up-to-the-minute competitive intelligence.

As you work with these Design Partners, bring them through how your product has evolved from concept to deliverable design. Share the data you've collected through *Ready* and *Aim,* and let them see how the data drives your vision. Do this to show them your objective approach to the market. If you let them know what your data told you the market needed and how you translated the data into features, they can follow your logic and lend some of their domain knowledge. The result? Features that are ever more relevant to the market you're targeting.

When you educate your Design Partners on your Market Validation process, you get two important benefits. First, customers and other supporters in the program gain confidence in what you're producing. As you turn to these Design Partners for early endorsements and case studies, they will be able to provide them with conviction.

The second benefit accrues through the effect on analysts, members of the press, and industry pundits. These constituencies are constantly approached to pontificate on the space you are entering. When you share your market data, they can call upon the data when sharing their opinions, and they can openly advocate the market-based approach you've educated them on. They're also more likely to endorse your product when the time comes. After all, if you've collected objective market data and shared the data openly to the point where you let them use some (not necessarily the conclusions that led to product features but the market data), how could they *not* be comfortable endorsing your approach when the time comes? What more could a fledgling product need than industry analysts espousing the objective approach your company took in developing its product?

RECRUIT PARTNERS ALL ALONG THE WAY

Whenever I conduct any type of interview during the *Aim* stage—whether by phone or in-person or with a potential customer, an analyst, or a member of the press—I'm always on the lookout for potential Design Partners. Every time I interact with someone, I'm listening for how much they know about the industry or market problem, how well they understand the business (versus more parochial self-interests that could be addressed by my product having the features only they would need), and probably most importantly, how articulate they are at communicating along all of this.

Usually, 10 to 20 percent of the people I've interacted with in the *Ready* and *Aim* phases fall into this category.

PARTNERS AS EARLY CUSTOMERS
AND TESTERS

A natural extension of the Design Partners Program is to make your Design Partners part of your product testing process. As products progress through development and into quality testing, frequently they are selectively released before general availability to the public, typically under nondisclosure agreements, to select users in the target audience for evaluation. Design Partners make an excellent audience for these prerelease products.

In my experience, you will need more customer testers than are available in your Design Partners Program. Moreover, many Design Partners are not hard-core users, as they may be part of the analyst or press community. But some of your Design Partners will be very useful as first testers. By now, they typically have a relationship with your company and will tend to overlook some of the early shortcomings of your development process.

EARLY PIPELINE

Progressing beyond testing, Design Partners make a natural base of first customers. They know the history of your company, have seen the product migrate from idea to tangible offering, and are often eager to be among the first actual users.

SOURCES OF PUBLIC RELATIONS CASE STUDIES AND MEDIA REFERENCES

The real advantage to Design Partners shows up as you get closer and closer to product release. You now have a ready base of users in your target audience, analysts who follow your market, and press contacts. They have been through the Design Partners Program and have seen the product progress from an idea to a tangible offering. As you move toward product launch, you have a ready basis of user stories, analyst references, and press that is already up to speed on your offering.

KEEPING THEM UP TO SPEED EFFICIENTLY

In closing out this section on Design Partners, let me describe what I have found to be the most efficient way to run this kind of program. Getting a product out the door while keeping abreast of the market is a difficult balancing act. You need to be efficient in your efforts while at the same time respectful of your Design Partners' time.

In my experience, you can expect to find 10 to 20 percent of your Market Validation contacts to be viable Design Partners. Not all of them will be interested, or they may not be willing to commit the time. I also have found it is not necessary to compensate them; in my experience, results were usually better with uncompensated Design Partners. Most people who are motivated to do this kind of work are interested in what your product can do for them. The opportunity to influence your product to better meet their needs is a powerful motivation and a truer indicator of genuine market pain.

In recruiting people for the program, it's important to let potential members know the time commitment on their part, along with the commitments on your company's part. Your commitment is to regularly deliver a current, usable, working version of the product or service (assuming this is possible) once it is stable enough to make this viable; each partner's commitment is to use the product in as close to a real-use setting as possible. As a company, you should include a very high level of support service response to facilitate real-world use. If you are fortunate enough to be able to deliver telephone support for your offering, this should include around-the-clock access. If service for your offering requires on-site visits, you should have clear protocols on how these resources can be accessed and the types of response times that can be expected. Remember, this level of support will give your Design Partners the confidence to use the product in more real-world settings. And that is what you're after.

Your support efforts at this stage should be viewed as an opportunity to see the product in real-world usage and to feed that valuable information back to the company. The Market Validation team must be kept abreast of how the product is being used and what types of support issues are being encountered. It is particularly valuable at this point in the development cycle to see what support issues are most common and to work to address them before the product is finalized. Many times, changes in a product during this phase can lead to substantially reduced support costs. A Design Partners Program is a great way to figure this out.

BOARDS OF ADVISORS

Design Partners Programs are put together to develop a formalized and efficient way to get real-world user input on your product as it goes through development on its way to being finalized. Members of these programs actually use the product or service in a day-to-day industrial or consumer setting. As the product nears finalization, they provide an excellent source of real-life usage examples and content for press articles, the analyst community, and company marketing materials.

During the *Ready* and *Aim* processes, you will have also uncovered numerous other buyers, beyond the users of the product, who are critical to the buying process. Typically, these multiperson buying teams are in business-buying environments versus consumer-buying situations. In these business environments, the larger the organization and the more expensive the product, the more buyers there are involved in the purchasing decision. In addition to the user-buyer, there can be those that install the product, pay for the product, manage the product, are responsible for its upkeep or maintenance, and have business responsibilities beyond straightforward day-to-day usage that are all involved in the decision-making process. Additionally, finance and legal organizations are often involved in the transaction part of the purchase. It is important that you know how these decision makers work and how they will react to the purchase of your product or service.

Buying decisions in business organizations are increasingly complex, and they involve more and more decision makers as the cost and criticality of the product increase. In addition, in lean times, these decision makers take on even more importance.

In my experience, the most efficient way to handle these complexities is through a program, similar to the Design Partners Program, which can gather a group of these decision makers together to help you efficiently understand their issues while the product is in development. The *Ready* and *Aim* processes have identified the types of decision makers specific to your product, and the Design Partners Program has brought together people, mostly user-buyers, who have a need for the product.

Now, you now need to develop a Board of Advisors Program. The goal here is to efficiently understand the management and executive decision-making that occurs around your product, the same way the Design Partners Program has done on the user end of things. In this case, you will be drawing from a broader constituent base to build your Board of Advisors. Some of these decision makers will be from the *Ready* and *Aim* steps, but as you continue to expand your market contacts, you should include other sources.

A Board of Advisors can educate your company on how decision makers think and what kinds of information will speed the decision-making process around the purchase of your product. For recruitment, you need to contact companies you have been working with and the various executive buyers you have been developing relationships with. Much like the Design Partners Program, if you have uncovered a real need in the market with associated real pain, compensation should not be needed for executives to join your Board of Advisors.

The outcomes you are after are identical to the Design Partners outcomes, but instead of representing potential *users* of the product, members of the Board of Advisors represent *decision makers* who decide whether to buy.

You administer this program slightly differently as well, since these constituents are typically not direct users of the offering. Instead of sending advisory board members the current version of your evolving product, you gather them in a room on a regular basis, update them on the product status, and get to know how the various decision makers evaluate the information to make a decision around your evolving offering. Some of their organizations may have others involved in the Design Partners Program and may be up to speed on the product development status; others may not.

I shoot for a Board of Advisors with twice as many participants as my Design Partners Program. This is because most business decisions involve two to three times as many decision makers as potential users. Again, some of your advisory board members will come from Design Partners companies; others will be recruited from companies not involved with Design Partners.

I have found the most effective way to run these programs is through regular group meetings. I shoot for every 30 days, with the expectation that 50 percent of the Board of Advisors in the city I am located in will show up. These meetings are best run in the window after the workday and before dinner—say, between 5:00 P.M. and 7:00 P.M. I'll take the first hour and update everyone on the status of the company, the state of development, and major changes to the product or company since the last meeting. For the remaining hour, I will cover current decisions the company is facing and ask for their input. This could include input on features, pricing, competition, or other issues related to product availability and readiness.

For remote advisory board members, I typically don't have as many meetings, because it tends to get inefficient. Any remote advisors usually have high leverage, meaning they are influential members of the press or analyst community that did not fit into the Design Partners Program.

The beauty of the Board of Advisors program is that like the Design Partners Program, it helps you build a constituency base of people who know your company and are up to speed on the issues the company is facing. As the company gets closer and closer to its ship date and needs more real-time input, you have a ready base of constituents; you can pick up the phone and get straight to the points you need to cover without taking the time required to educate them on the status of the company.

CHAPTER TWENTY-ONE

Showtime

Launch, Market, and Sell the Product

Okay, so it's time for the big show—the event for which all this Market Validation time, effort, and energy has been spent: It's time for product launch and your first year of sales and marketing. You must view these two as integral events. As I have advocated again and again throughout this book, the complete Market Validation process requires that you follow through on all your market-based design efforts and deliver a product to market with a full-on launch and first-year sales and marketing effort.

In today's world, with its 65 percent product failure rates, you *must* follow this advice to give your offering its fair shot in the market. The best product or service in the world will not see the light of day without substantive sales and marketing efforts.

The purpose of this book, and in particular this section, is not to provide a full primer on new service launches and sales and marketing programs. I'll review some of the top-level issues surrounding these topics, with an eye toward showing you how to make them even more productive based on your Market Validation efforts to date.

LAUNCH

Launch for a new product is a one-time event, where the light will shine on your product for a brief moment. This is your offering's 15 minutes of fame. There are no second chances. I love to use the metaphor in which an elephant is charging you, and you have an elephant gun with one gigantic bullet in it. You will feel the pressure from all over to shoot quickly, but as you know by now, the secret is to take your time, remember the results of all your efforts to date, get ready, take careful aim, and when ready, fire. Given you only have one bullet to shoot, be sure you shoot at the right time. You have one chance for your offering to have its 15 minutes of fame, so make sure it's the right 15 minutes. In the world of product launches, there simply are no do-overs.

EXTENSIVE KNOWLEDGE BASED ON EFFORTS

The first thing to remember at launch time is the extensive amount of work you've done in the *Ready, Aim,* and *Fire* stages of Market Validation. Your level of expertise and market knowledge is far superior to anyone else's. Some analysts might know more about certain *segments* of the market, and some competitors might have deeper knowledge on other areas, but in aggregate, if you've done Market Validation right, no one can match your knowledge base. You need to exploit this as you launch your product.

Every piece of information you've gathered throughout this process is designed to give you a more effective product in the market, and this is reflected in your offering. Now, you need to go out and educate the market on this, in the same way you've done it with your Design Partners and Board of Advisors. Part of the beauty of these programs is the practice they give you in educating your market on your product and in understanding customers' buying processes. This knowledge is absolutely invaluable as you approach the big launch event.

EARLY CUSTOMERS, SUCCESS STORIES

The key payoffs of the *Fire* phase of Market Validation are the jump starts you have with customers. First, you have a set of customers from your Design Partners and advisory board members who are familiar with your offering, know the fact-based approach you used to develop the product, and can serve as references to the press and analyst community. In the end, nothing builds credibility with analysts and the press like someone else singing your company's praises; when these supporters are your customers, the credibility is even higher.

Another major benefit is all the contact you have from your Market Validation efforts. Not only is this a set of customers that fit your target market and are familiar with your product, but you also understand your target market, what types of companies or demographics they come from, and how to find more of them on a reproducible basis. The key point for ongoing success is a targeted market that you can develop to create sustained demand for your product.

CYCLE BACK TO INFLUENCERS FROM EARLIER CHAPTERS

As you get closer and closer to your ship date, you should cycle back to all the people you have contacted throughout your Market Validation efforts and update them on the status of your product and its pending launch. Those in your target audience have some knowledge of your product based on their interactions with you. They should be contacted as you approach launch to reacquaint them with your offering and its availability.

Other influencers that you have worked with in the past, those from press and analyst communities, and pundits in general should also be updated.

In all cases, you might want to offer some level of reduced price or early delivery based on the help they have lent you. An important note: There's no need to take the incentive too far; a decent price discount, or quick delivery if allocations are an issue, should suffice. Offer much beyond this, and you need to question the level of market pain you are addressing.

SUSTAINED SALES AND MARKETING EFFORTS

I've been preaching this throughout the book, and mercifully, I promise this is the last time! Remember, in today's world, no product sells itself. You must get out and aggressively sell and market it.

The goal of this book is not to educate you on sales and marketing but to educate you on how important it is do both of them well. The generic indicator of these efforts that can be used across industries and company sizes is the ratio of spending on your product development efforts to the first-year launch and sales and marketing efforts. These need to be a solid one-to-one ratio; the monetary investment in designing and building your product needs to equal the monetary investment in your first-year launch and sales and marketing efforts.

MARKET VALIDATION AS A
CULTURAL ATTRIBUTE

Market Validation, with its three steps of *Ready, Aim,* and *Fire,* is a culture, not a one-time effort. Once started, it perpetuates itself for as long as the product is in the market. After you've released your product, it is critical to continue the Market Validation process for the next release.

Once you've used the process for one offering, it will typically permeate an organization for all of its new offerings. Once that new offering is out the door, continue the process for the rapid-fire product iterations that gain you more and more market share in more and more submarkets.

Once you've covered a fair number of submarkets, raise your sights to the overall market. Build on the supporting domination of the base markets to own an entire category.

In today's world, if you're not doing this, someone else will.

CHAPTER TWENTY-TWO
The *Fire* Checklist

Here are the summary points for the *Fire* process. This is the final step of the Market Validation process that gets your offering into the market.

I. SALES AND MARKETING: BUDGET FOR IT

In today's brutally competitive and crowded markets, customers do not find your product; your job is to find them. Regardless of the attributes and the competitive advantage in your offering, you must properly allocate the budget and resources needed to get your product into the market with a successful launch and then follow on with a full year's sales and marketing budget.

To accomplish this, allocate an equivalent amount of funding for your first-year launch, sales, and marketing efforts as you do for product development. If you are working on a fixed budget, reallocate on this 50/50 basis to assure all your Market Validation efforts receive proper follow-through on the sales and marketing execution front.

2. THE DETAILS: WRITE PRODUCT SPECS AND SCHEDULES

Once you have accumulated all the information from your Market Validation efforts, you need to document how these translate into product features and in turn create a schedule to develop those features into a finished offering.

Market Validation team members usually have skill sets falling into one of two categories: sales and marketing or research and development. Within these skill sets, the sales and marketing team needs to develop a PRD, or Product Requirements Document, clearly outlining how the Market Validation results are translated into features and functionality. The research and development team needs to sign off on this document, indicating they understand the feature descriptions and how they were arrived at based on the Market Validation results.

Once the PRD is complete, the research and development team needs to break down each of the product features and functions into a development schedule with corresponding time frames. This document, in turn, is signed off by the sales and marketing team. This leads to the interdependence of the two teams on each other and on the Market Validation results, ensuring that a properly specified product is shipped within a given time frame.

3. FAST TO MARKET: GET A MARKET-ORIENTED PRODUCT OUT QUICKLY

Once the product specification and ship schedule are known, it is critical to get the product out quickly. At this critical phase, any interesting market is constantly changing, and the team must move as expeditiously as possible to ship the offering.

There are many techniques to employ here. They include shipping the minimally acceptable feature set, shipping multiple releases of your product using fast release iterations, shipping only must-have—versus nice-to-have—features, shipping products where the quality assurance process has focused on high usage patterns, and killing features early in the development process.

All of these techniques lead to getting your product out as quickly as possible to get the ultimate form of Market Validation: customers voting for your product with their money.

4. EARLY CUSTOMERS: RECRUIT DESIGN PARTNERS AND ADVISORY BOARDS

The most effective way both to get real-world input on your product as you're developing it and to recruit early customers is to run both a Design Partners Program and a Board of Advisors.

Design Partners are end-users of your product who you keep up to speed on the progress of your development. Let them use your product or service offering in real-world environments as it is under development so that you can capture real-world usage scenarios, understand how your target market will actually use the product, and get them familiar with the offering. As you transition to shipping the final offering, you have a ready base of usage scenarios, case studies, and potential customers.

Advisory boards typically are put together for commercial offerings when there are many decision makers involved in the buying process. These members are not so much end users as department managers, people who pay for the offering, maintain it, install it, or manage the budgets and contracts for it. These individuals give you real-world input as to how they view the decision-making process for your product as you get closer and closer to launch. Here again, you have a ready supply of usage scenarios, case studies, and potential customers.

5. SHOWTIME: LAUNCH, MARKET, AND SELL THE PRODUCT

It is time for the big show—the launch and the first year of marketing and sales; time for all that Market Validation effort to come together and show its value. You've done the work: produced the product, obtained early endorsements, recruited early customers, and achieved a full understanding of the target audience and how to reach them.

The critical point now is to fully execute a well-funded launch, sales, and marketing campaign. As covered earlier, the key to all this is to make sure your launch, sales, and marketing budget equals your development budget.

It is time to watch the market's reaction to your new product or service!

The critical follow-through is this: Keep up your Market Validation efforts as the product gains acceptance. And continue to ship all your new products and services using a Market Validation approach.

The only way to succeed in today's markets is to make Market Validation a cultural attribute.

ABOUT THE AUTHOR

Rob Adams is an active investor, author, consultant, and staff member of the Management Department at the University of Texas at Austin's McCombs School of Business, where he teaches in the MBA program and is the Director of the Global Moot Corp Program.

Dr. Adams is an active angel investor and board member for several start-ups, and he is affiliated with numerous venture funds, several of which he started. Prior to the venture business, he was a software operating executive for two decades. Throughout his venture and operating careers he has been a founder, founding investor, or involved with the public offering, merger, or acquisition of more than 40 companies, representing the launching of more than 100 products, and transactions totaling more than one billion dollars of capital.

Prior to his appointment at the University of Texas, Adams founded Tejas Venture Partners, the second venture fund he has started. Previously, he was the founder of AV Labs, a successful early stage venture fund allied with Austin Ventures, starting it after being a partner with TL Ventures. Before entering the venture business, he was a technology executive. He started his career with Lotus (NYSE: IBM), joining the company shortly after its public offering. Adams was instrumental in the development and launch of both 1-2-3 for Macintosh and Lotus Notes. He went on to be founder and CEO of Business Matters, a venture-backed developer of financial modeling products, and was an executive with Pervasive Software (NASDAQ: PVSW), a company he helped take public.

Adams holds a Bachelor of Science degree in Engineering from Purdue University, where he is a Distinguished Alumnus, a Masters of Business Administration from Babson College's Olin School of Management, and a PhD in Management from Capella University. He has taught at the MBA programs of The Acton School of Business, Babson College, The University of Texas at Austin, and St. Edwards University.

He is a nationally recognized expert and speaker on entrepreneurship, company and product strategy, marketing and technology issues. He recently keynoted the Inc. 500 business conference and consults for numerous Fortune 500 companies. He provides expert testimony on technology-related business issues, and he has consulted on economic development and early stage company development for numerous governments including Chile, Costa Rica, India, Malaysia, New Zealand, and Thailand. He has been covered in *BusinessWeek*, *Forbes*, *Fortune*, *Money*, the *New York Times*, the *Wall Street Journal*, *Washington Post*, on Bloomberg Radio, Public Television, and public radio's nationally syndicated *Marketplace* program.

He is the author of *A Good Hard Kick in the Ass: Basic Training for Entrepreneurs* (New York: Random House/Crown, 2002).

Adams is a Fellow at the IC2 Institute, a University of Texas–based foundation that runs the Austin Technology Incubator, on the board of Purdue Research Park, and a volunteer with Austin's Habitat for Humanity. He is an avid downhill skier and marathoner. He was a collegiate rower and graduated from the Marine Corps' Officer Candidate School.

For more information go to www.drrobadams.com.

Index